MEDITERRANEAN COOKING

HILAIRE WALDEN

MEDITERRANEAN COOKING

HILAIRE WALDEN

PHOTOGRAPHY BY JAMES MERRELL

According to geographers, hunched, gnarled olive trees mark the boundaries of the Mediterranean zone, but to most people it is a region of azure blue seas, piercingly blue skies, clear bright light, ochre and gray soil, brilliantly whitewashed houses with rose or rusty-gold colored roofs, beaded curtains at the doors and shutters at the windows. Therefore, the region includes eastern Spain, southern France, Italy, Greece, Turkey, Syria, Israel, Lebanon, Jordan, Egypt, Libya, Tunisia, Algeria and eastern Morocco. Although these countries are so obviously divergent in their peoples, lifestyles, political systems, cultures and religions, they still have an inescapable similarity when it comes to food.

Flavors, ingredients and cooking methods are repeated from country to country. You'll find olive oil, garlic, onions, tomatoes, eggplants, peppers, fruits, plenty of herbs and spices, country breads, fish and poultry, the smoky flavor of charcoal-broiled foods and thick omelet "cakes," such as frittatas, slowly cooked and packed full of vegetables. Each country also shares the pleasant practice of idly nibbling from inviting displays of small tempting dishes before a meal.

Colorful and varied, Mediterranean cooking is flavored and scented with anything that will add taste or aroma, from garlic to rose buds. It emanates from the homes of ordinary people, where the best real Mediterranean food is to be found, and is simple and unpretentious. It has a freedom that allows each cook to add his or her own, often secret touches, yet at the same time, it is rooted in tradition and unaffected by fashion or fads.

The people of the Mediterranean attach great importance to food and it is prepared with pleasure and pride for the delight and well-being of family and friends. Eating is a relaxed and sociable occasion because people enjoy food and love to share it; visitors are automatically provided with something to eat or drink.

The average Mediterranean diet has recently been acclaimed for its healthiness. Olive oil is the predominant fat (it is even used on bread instead of butter), while the use of butter and cream is severely limited. Quantities of meat are small, but fish and shellfish are enormously popular. Grains, beans, bread, herbs, vegetables and fruit are eaten in large quantities. Broiling, roasting and slow simmering are the most popular cooking methods.

The countries of the Mediterranean all have a similar climate: dry hot summers and mild winters, rare but violent rainstorms and strong winds – with slight variations according to latitude, thus similar crops are grown throughout the region. The climate also accounts for a shortage of pasture, so livestock is restricted mainly to sheep, goats, poultry and, where allowed by religion, pigs. Since there is a dearth of cows' milk, cheese, cream and butter, Mediterranean cheeses and yogurts are more commonly made from ewes' and goats' milk, although exceptions are found in central and northern Italy.

Over thousands of years, there has been a tremendous interchange of peoples, religions and customs as a result of colonization, migration, invasion, counter-invasion and trading. It is therefore inevitable that similar dishes will be served in a number of countries. However, there has been so much intermingling of peoples that it is a futile task to try to find the origin, if indeed there is one, for many of them. Dolmades, with variations in both name and ingredients, are found from the Middle East to Greece; Middle Eastern Tarator (page 25) and Greek Skorthalia (page 23) are similar garlic sauces thickened with a purée of nuts, while Spinach with Raisins and Pine Nuts (page 59) is eaten in Spain, Italy and Arab countries. Therefore, where there could be confusion in name or spelling, I have used English names.

Mediterranean Cooking includes a whole range of typical regional recipes. The book begins with a selection of recipes for soups and sauces. All over the Mediterranean, soups tend to be hearty and sustaining, for example, Soupe au Pistou (page 17). In the south of France, this sort of soup plays such a major role in the diet that the evening meal has become known as "le souper." Perhaps the most ubiquitous Mediterranean soup, however, is fish soup and every region of every country has its own version. Many originated as fishermen's dishes – cooked on their boats as they made their way back to port or when they came ashore, using the fish which were too small or too insignificant to sell.

Either as an integral part of a dish or served separately, sauces are popular everywhere. Mediterranean cooks do not use flour to thicken their sauces – the thickening agent is more usually ground nuts, bread crumbs or even mashed potatoes. Many sauces are cold, using oil as the liquid. Pesto (page 23) is often referred to as a sauce, but actually has a soft, light spreadable consistency, and Anchoïade (page 21) and Tapenade (page 23), too, are spreads or pastes. Although perhaps not traditional, puréed mezzes such as Eggplant Dip (page 36), may be served as a sauce with broiled or baked meat or fish, or tossed with pasta.

The serving of tapas, antipasti and mezze is a typically Mediterranean custom. These dishes are usually savory, mildly sharp with lemon juice or vinegar, piquant with capers or olives, aromatic with herbs or fragrant with spices or garlic. All the dishes are served together for everyone to help themselves to whatever they like, when they like. There need not be a grand spread; a few simple items, such as Marinated Olives (page 29), salted fresh whole almonds or slices of Parma ham or jamón serrano (Spanish air-cured ham) will be quite enough, particularly at home.

Recently it has become popular to serve one of these individual dishes alone as a first course, a selection of dishes for a simple lunch or supper, or an even wider choice for parties and buffets. Choose from a colorful selection, with varied tastes and textures, such as purées, crisp raw salads, broiled vegetables, cold dressed beans, or herby marinated cheeses, fish and meats – all accompanied by some of the good fresh bread for which the region is renowned.

Eggs are used extensively around the Mediterranean region, in omelets and eggahs, tortillas and frittatas – some so substantial that they can be wrapped up and taken off to the fields to feed the farm workers for lunch. Eggs are also popular scrambled with tomatoes and peppers to make Chakchouka (page 46) or Piperade (page 48), or served hard-boiled with mayonnaise, Aïoli or Al-i-oli (page 24). As for cheese, because cattle are scarce throughout the Mediterranean, cheeses are invariably made from ewes', goats' or water buffaloes' milk.

Vegetables bring color to the Mediterranean markets and diet. Chosen with care and eaten with relish, vegetables play a major part in many dishes, often sufficiently substantial to constitute the main part of the meal, replacing meat dishes altogether. Religious restrictions have also played a part in elevating the role of vegetables. In Christian countries, especially in earlier times, many people abstain from eating meat during the long Lenten fast, as well as on holy days and Fridays. The Greek Orthodox Church also bans meat-eating on certain days. Consequently, cooks have learned how to make the very best of each vegetable to create what is now a rich repertoire of dishes.

When it comes to fish, some of the best in the world can be found in the region. Mediterraneans love their fish fresh and simply cooked, preferably over an open fire with nothing more than fresh herbs, a drizzle of good olive oil and lemon juice to bring out the flavor.

Meat, on the other hand, is at a premium, and so is highly respected and cooked in the most sympathetic and quality-enhancing ways. Climate and religion dictate that lamb is the type of meat most often eaten. Sheep and goats are more common in this region than cattle. Veal is popular, and pork is eaten in Greece, Cyprus and in Italy, but of course is forbidden by the religious laws of Judaism and Islam. Rabbit, hare and, above all, wild boar are prized by the passionate hunters of France and Italy, while domestic rabbits and chickens are raised by householders all over the region.

Beans, grains and products made from them, such as bread and pasta, all feature prominently in Mediterranean diets. Beans are a good source of protein, and those such as chick peas and lentils go into dips, sauces and casseroles. Rice is not usually served plainly boiled. Instead, it is first turned in hot oil then mixed together with herbs, spices, nuts, vegetables, seafood, meats, beans or other grains. Perhaps the best-known of all these rice dishes is Risotto (page 108), with its different variations.

Pasta is always associated with Italy, but many other Mediterranean countries have their own pastas, such as the Spanish fideos. Wheat is not only the ingredient used for making pasta, but also used in couscous, a type of fine semolina, particularly associated with North Africa but also enjoyed in other Arab countries. Bread is an important staple in the Mediterranean diet and every country has its own repertoire of breads.

Finally, the Middle Eastern sweet tooth is legendary and echoed by that of the Turks and the Greeks. The very sweet recipes for which they are renowned are not eaten at the end of a meal, but served with coffee when entertaining and on special occasions. Mediterranean meals usually end with fresh fruit of which there is a colorful, fragrant and luscious abundance. This does not mean that desserts are never made. They do, however, tend to be simple and homely.

So while there are many local ingredients and recipes common to the different countries bordering the Mediterranean, of course – and thank goodness – each country does have its own special flavors.

Spain, for example, is closer to North Africa and the Middle East than other European countries in its cooking as well as geographically, and uses spices more than herbs – parsley being the only one quite widely used. Provençal dishes are redolent of wild herbs, anchovies, olives, orange peel and especially basil. This herb continues to star throughout Italy, where it is joined by rosemary, tarragon, parsley, sage, thyme and marjoram. In Greece, oregano, dill, parsley, lemon, cinnamon and allspice flavor the cooking, while Turks use dill, parsley, cinnamon and allspice. Throughout the Middle East, parsley and mint are the popular herbs and cumin is a characteristic spice. Egyptian cooks also like cinnamon, while the fiery chile-based paste, harissa, typifies the cooking of Tunisia and, to a lesser extent, that of Algeria.

When making my recipes, I hope you will follow the ethos of Mediterranean cooks and adjust the flavors and ingredients to your taste or according to availability.

Hilaire Walden

EQUIPMENT

Although each country has its own special utensils, there are many that are common to all, and easily available elsewhere. These include a selection of heavy-bottomed frying pans, good quality sharp knives and the cornerstone of so many Mediterranean recipes, at least one pestle and mortar. The end of a rolling pin in a bowl often makes the best alternative, as I have indicated in the relevant recipes.

I have mentioned food processors or blenders only where I think they will do. A vegetable mill with two or more different-sized screens is the best piece of equipment for puréeing soups and vegetables, especially potatoes, removing skins from cooked fruits, such as apples, pears and peaches, and seeds from berries.

Heavy glazed and unglazed earthenware pots and casserole dishes, such as Spanish cazuelas, which can go in the oven and on the cook top and retain the heat well, are favored for long, slow simmering; where no lid is available, improvise with a tight covering of aluminum foil. Unglazed pots are also reputed to give food a special flavor.

Earthenware pots must be seasoned before use for the first time or they will crack. To do this, half-fill with cold water and a good splash of vinegar, bring slowly to a boil and leave to boil until the liquid has evaporated.

Tin-lined copper is also popular as it has similar heat-retaining properties. Enamelled cast-iron ware offers a cheaper alternative.

SPECIAL EQUIPMENT

These items are used for specific dishes and you may like to have have one or two pieces for added authenticity, but the recipes can be made using other equipment.

Italian kitchens have a special knife for slicing Parmesan cheese (a sharp potato peeler may be used instead), a good cheese grater, a very large saucepan for cooking pasta, and a mezzaluna – a sickle-shaped, doubled-handled blade that is very useful for chopping fresh herbs.

DAUBIERE

A French plump, earthenware pot for cooking casseroles. A daubière has a shallow lid that is filled with cold water or ice so the aromatic steam rising from the casserole quickly condenses and drips on to the meat and vegetables to keep them moist. Daubières are now difficult to find, but a sturdy enamelled cast-iron equivalent, doufeau, can be used quite successfully instead.

MOROCCAN TAGINE

A shallow, round earthenware pot with a tall, conical lid like a Chinese coolie's hat, that can be put on a low heat providing it contains some liquid, and is used for slow-cooked stews. An ordinary heavy casserole dish will suffice.

BEAN POTS

These have rounded bodies with narrower openings at the top and close-fitting lids. Traditionally, they were nestled in the fire and because of their shape, beans cooked in them lost very little moisture by evaporation.

COUSCOUSSIER

This may be made from unglazed earthenware, tin-lined copper or aluminum and is traditionally used for cooking couscous, but it is not necessary with the pre-cooked grain that is now available. A couscoussier comes in two parts – a lower pot in which the meat or vegetable part of the recipe is cooked, and an upper section with a perforated base to hold the grain. The aromatic steam from the stew permeates through the holes to heat and flavor the grain above.

PAELLA PANS

These are round and made of iron, with two looped handles opposite each other, a flat base of a good thickness, and shallow, sloping sides. They should be wide enough to allow the rice to be cooked in a single layer and proportioned so the water required to cook the rice comes up to the edge of the pan handles. A very large frying pan is second best and only feasible for paellas for a small number of people – a 14 inch pan is adequate for only 3-4 people.

Before using a traditional iron paella pan for the first time, to avoid the first paella having a metallic flavor, wash the pan very carefully in a mixture of vinegar and fine sand, then rinse it and wash normally in hot, soapy water. Dry the pan thoroughly.

Brushing with a coating of oil between use is often recommended as a preventative measure against rusting, but I prefer to dust the pan with an even covering of flour because if there is a long time lapse before another paella is made, oil may become rancid.

BAKEWARE

For useful bakeware for breads and pizzas, see the information on page 111.

INGREDIENTS

Shops now stock a much wider selection of products. Until a few years ago, items such as couscous were rare except in ethnic shops, but they are now sold even in supermarkets. There are also many more specialist shops. Many of the ingredients, especially in supermarkets, are mass-produced, which inevitably means not of the best quality, but the availability of traditional, good-quality products is widening hearteningly, allowing us to produce dishes that more closely resemble the authentic versions.

When travelling, do buy local produce – cheeses, nuts, beans, dried fruits, olives, salted anchovies and capers, and whole spices from Middle Eastern and North African souks. They have a stronger flavor than those sold in this country.

ANCHOVIES

I prefer salted whole anchovies rather than fillets canned in oil, as they have a superior flavor. Before using salted anchovies, they should be washed, scaled if necessary, the bones carefully removed and discarded and then dried. If they taste too salty, soak them in milk for about 30 minutes.

BURGHUL

Also called bulgur in Turkey and pourgouri in Greece, this is made from hulled wheat grains, cracked by boiling and then dried. You must rehydrate it before use, either by soaking for about 20 minutes, or by simmering for a couple of minutes. The grains must then be drained and squeezed hard to expel excess moisture. Burghul makes an interesting, foolproof and quick alternative to rice and can be flavored in the same ways as pilaf-type dishes. Use a fine grained variety for tabbouleh and kibbeh, and a coarse one for pilafs.

CAPERS

Salted capers can be bought around the Mediterranean and in a few specialist shops over here. They have a fresher flavor and better texture than capers packed in brine (the salt easily rinses off).

CHEESE

The range of genuine cheeses rather than "look-alikes" is widening encouragingly.

Buffalo milk mozzarella – genuine mozzarella is made from water buffaloes' milk and has a more pronounced yet delicate, fresher and more fragrant flavor than the more common cows' milk version. It is also more compact, fairly elastic, whiter and will ooze "tears" of whey when cut.

Halumi – a firm, white, creamy, mild-flavored cheese, similar in flavor to feta, but less salty. A favorite cheese in Greece, Cyprus, and Lebanon where it is often flavored with cumin seeds. In Cyprus ewes' milk is traditionally used.

Kefalotiri – a hard, salty ewes' or goats' milk cheese that is good for grating and cooking. **Parmesan** can be substituted.

Ricotta – made from the whey left after making other cheeses, it should be eaten very fresh when it has a delicate, clean, fresh taste; it quickly develops an acidic bitter edge.

COUSCOUS

Made from semolina that has been ground, moistened and rolled in flour. Most couscous is now pre-cooked and needs only to be moistened and steamed to heat through and separate the grains. Butter is usually rubbed into the couscous to help the grains to separate and to enrich them.

HERBS

With the exception of oregano and rigani, use fresh herbs – they give a truer flavor than dried ones. Even so, the flavor can vary quite considerably, so it is important to taste each batch and adjust the quantity used. It is easy to grow a few plants in window boxes positioned in a sunny spot. Keep freshly cut herbs in "stay fresh" bags available from health food stores and some supermarkets. Freeze them in small quantities. I have never dried herbs to my satisfaction in a microwave. If fresh herbs are an impossibility, use freeze-dried or frozen herbs rather than dried.

Mint – the most widely used variety is spearmint.

Oregano/Rigani – picked when the flowers are in bud, and then dried. The hot, dry climate of Greece gives them just a little more pungency, so buy in bunches or stripped from the stalk from Greek food shops. Home-grown oregano should be allowed to dry for a few hours before using.

Parsley – use the flat-leaved continental variety.

OLIVE OIL

Credited with playing an important part in the healthiness of the Mediterranean diet, it is excellent for cooking as it can be heated to high temperatures and will seal the outside of food, preventing the oil being absorbed.

There is now a burgeoning range of olive oils of different styles and qualities. The descending order of quality, purity, intensity of flavor and price of the grades are as follows:

Extra virgin oil – from the first pressing of the olives, this has the lowest acidity and the most rounded flavor. Commercially produced extra virgin oils are blended from oils of differing character and quality, and will always taste the same. Extra-virgin oils from estates, farms and village co-operatives have their own individual characters and, as they are unblended, will vary from year to year in the same way as the best wines.

Virgin oil – results from the second pressing of the olives.

Simple "olive oil" – or "pure olive oil" – a blend of virgin olive oil and refined oils obtained by chemical extraction.

Extra-virgin oil is used in salads or for when only small quantities of oil are required. Virgin oil is used in salads or more widely in cooking, and simple olive oil for cooking.

Flavors and colors of olive oils from different countries – and even from different areas – vary from delicate and grassy to full, heavy and fruity. Spanish oils tend to be lighter than Italian ones, whereas Greek oils are even heavier, because the olives become very ripe before being picked. Color is no indication of quality – a rich dark green does not necessarily mean a superior oil, although it is an indication of the strength of flavor. Store olive oil in a cool, dark place, but not in the refrigerator.

OLIVES

If you have visited a Mediterranean food market, you will know that olives come in many different varieties and colors; cured in brine, packed in oil, or flavored with herbs, spices and lemon. Color differences are linked to ripeness – a progression from green, through yellow or greeny brown, to red, violet, then purple and black. Olives sold loose in barrels are generally of a more reliable quality.

PEPPERS

Charring the skin produces a magical transformation in the flavor of the flesh. Char peppers over a hot barbecue, or halve, flatten and place under a preheated very hot broiler, or in a preheated oven. After charring, leave until cool enough to handle, then peel off the skin with a sharp knife.

PROSCIUTTO

Prosciutto crudo, usually labelled just "prosciutto," is cured and salted raw ham. Made throughout Italy, various styles and qualities are available. Parma ham, which can only be made according to strict regulations around Parma, is generally considered the best, although some *aficionados* prefer San Daniele.

SAFFRON

Use pure saffron threads in preference to the powder which may have been adulterated. A mere pinch of saffron is all that is needed to flavor a dish for 4-6 people, so threads are not as expensive as they may first seem. Gently and lightly toasting the saffron threads in a dry, heavy frying pan will bring out the flavor, and crushing them before adding to a dish will help them to dissolve more quickly.

SPICES

To walk around a spice souk is a heady and memorable experience. All around are large sacks brimming with mostly unidentifiable pods, seeds, buds, berries, roots and pieces of bark of varying hues, all exuding their own special fragrance, creating an exhilarating sensuous mélange. These spices are fresh and so have a stronger "fresher" flavor than many sold here. It really is important not to store spices for long and to always keep them in a cool, dark place. I buy whole spices (except nutmeg) then grind them to order, after first dry-roasting them in a heavy frying pan for a minute or so.

SUN-DRIED TOMATOES

Choose plump, well-flavored tomatoes, dried naturally under the hot Mediterranean sun. Cheap ones won't be genuine. Sun-dried tomatoes preserved in olive oil are more expensive than those in the dry form. The latter should be soaked in hot water for 1-1½ hours then dried with paper towels before using. To have a supply ready for use, soak several at a time then layer them in a jar with olive oil, seal and keep in a cool place. The oil from sun-dried tomatoes is ideal in salads and for brushing on crostinis and pizzas.

TOMATOES

The dire situation of flavorless, woolly tomatoes is being redressed, as most supermarkets now offer tomatoes "grown for flavor." Good tomatoes imported from Mediterranean countries are more easily available, too. To skin and seed tomatoes, pour boiling water over them, leave for 2-3 minutes, drain and slip off the skins when they are cool enough to handle. Cut in half and scoop out the seeds.

TAHINI

Also spelt "tahina," this is a paste made from ground toasted sesame seeds. Brands differ in their flavor, so it may be worth trying a number to find one you like. Tahini separates if left to stand for a while and must be stirred thoroughly before using; I usually invert the jar for a while to make blending easier. Keep tahini in a cool place, but preferably not the refrigerator as this makes blending more difficult.

YOGURT

Greek strained ewes' milk yogurt is the type used in the southern and eastern Mediterranean and is now quite readily available here. It has a unique, mild creamy flavor with just a hint of acidity. Strained cows' milk yogurt falls short of this and ordinary cows' milk yogurt further still.

Soups & Sauces

Throughout the Mediterranean, soups tend to be hearty and sustaining, packed with dried beans, lentils, rice, pasta and vegetables. Served with plenty of bread for dipping, many are complete meals in themselves. Mediterranean sauces are more usually thickened with pulverized nuts or bread crumbs than with flour. They may be an integral part of a dish or a separate entity; and some sauces are used more as spreads or pastes, or mixed with cream or soft cheese to make a sauce for pasta.

GAZPACHO

A bowl of chilled, colorful Gazpacho is one of the glories of Andalusian cooking and the epitome of hot weather food. Some sources claim that the soup dates back to before Roman times, others that it originated during the struggles against the Moorish invaders, but it could not have existed in the form we know it until after the sixteenth century when peppers and tomatoes were introduced to Spain. Gazpacho used to be served after the main course and before the fruit, but now its usual place is at the beginning of the meal. There are many recipes for Gazpacho, the varying proportions of ingredients resulting in endless changes of color and taste. The success of any version, however, depends on the quality of the ingredients and on not allowing one flavor to dominate.

1½ LB EXTRA LARGE TOMATOES, SKINNED, DESEEDED AND DICED

½ SPANISH ONION, CHOPPED

1 SWEET GREEN PEPPER, CORED, DESEEDED AND CHOPPED

1 SWEET RED PEPPER, CORED, DESEEDED AND CHOPPED

2 CLOVES OF GARLIC, CHOPPED

2 SLICES OF FIRM WHITE BREAD, CRUSTS REMOVED, BROKEN INTO PIECES

1¼ CUPS TOMATO JUICE

3 TABLESPOONS VIRGIN OLIVE OIL

2 TABLESPOONS SHERRY VINEGAR

SALT AND PEPPER

ICE CUBES TO SERVE

ACCOMPANIMENTS

1 SMALL SWEET RED PEPPER, CORED, DESEEDED AND DICED

1 SMALL SWEET GREEN PEPPER, CORED, DESEEDED AND DICED

1 SMALL ONION, DICED

1 HARD-BOILED EGG, CHOPPED

CROUTONS (SEE NEXT RECIPE)

Put all the soup ingredients, except the ice cubes, in a food processor or blender. Mix until smooth, then pour through a nylon strainer, pressing down well on the contents of the strainer. If necessary, thin the soup with a little water, then chill well.

Place the accompaniments in separate bowls. Adjust the seasoning of the soup, if necessary, then pour into cold soup bowls. Add a few ice cubes to each bowl and serve with the accompaniments.

Serves 4

Overleaf:
Clockwise from top: Gazpacho,
Broiled Mediterranean Vegetable Soup
and Soupe au Pistou

BROILED MEDITERRANEAN VEGETABLE SOUP

Featuring broiled eggplant, red peppers, tomatoes, garlic and herbs, this is for me the quintessential Mediterranean soup and one of my favorites, especially in summer. I do not bother to remove the seeds from the tomatoes, as they add interest to the soup's appearance.

1 LARGE ONION, HALVED BUT NOT PEELED

4 CLOVES OF GARLIC

4 RIPE BUT FIRM TOMATOES

2 EGGPLANTS, TOTAL WEIGHT 1½ LB, HALVED LENGTHWAYS

2 SWEET RED PEPPERS, HALVED

3 TABLESPOONS VIRGIN OLIVE OIL, PLUS EXTRA FOR BRUSHING

5 SPRIGS OF THYME

1 FRESH BAY LEAF, TORN

4-5 HALVES OF SUN-DRIED TOMATOES, CHOPPED

6 CUPS GOOD CHICKEN OR VEGETABLE STOCK

6 LARGE BASIL LEAVES, TORN

LEMON JUICE TO TASTE

SALT AND PEPPER

TO SERVE

3 SLICES OF COUNTRY BREAD (SEE PAGE 113), CRUSTS REMOVED

OLIVE OIL

TORN BASIL LEAVES (OPTIONAL)

Cook the onion, garlic, ripe tomatoes, eggplants and peppers under a preheated hot broiler until charred and softened. Cool slightly, then peel the onion, garlic and tomatoes. Remove the charred patches from the eggplants and red peppers and discard the pepper cores and seeds. Roughly chop them all.

Gently heat the olive oil with the thyme and bay leaf for a few minutes. Add the chopped vegetables, sun-dried tomatoes and stock, bring to a boil, cover and simmer gently for 20 minutes. Add the basil and simmer for a further 5 minutes. Cool slightly, then purée briefly in a blender or food processor at slow speed to retain some pieces of eggplant skin and pepper. Return to the pan, season and add lemon juice to taste. Reheat, but the soup is best if it is not too hot when eaten.

Just before serving, make the croutons. Brush the bread with oil, cut into cubes and bake in a preheated oven, 400°F, until crisp and golden. Serve the soup garnished with basil and accompanied by the croutons.

Serves 4-6

SOUPE AU PISTOU

This aromatic soup resembles a minestrone with pistou, a type of pesto without pine nuts, added at the end.

½ CUP DRIED SOISSONS OR CANNELLINI BEANS, SOAKED
OVERNIGHT AND DRAINED

3 TABLESPOONS OLIVE OIL

2 LEEKS, WHITE PART ONLY, THINLY SLICED

2 CARROTS, CHOPPED

½ LB PUMPKIN, DESEEDED, PEELED AND COARSELY DICED

I CUP FAVA BEANS

I CUP GREEN BEANS, CUT INTO 3-4 INCH PIECES

I ZUCCHINI, CUT INTO CHUNKS

4 TOMATOES, SKINNED, DESEEDED AND CHOPPED

¼ CUP DRIED ELBOW MACARONI OR SHELL PASTA

SALT AND PEPPER

PISTOU

⅔ CUP BASIL LEAVES

2 CLOVES OF GARLIC

½ CUP Parmesan CHEESE, FRESHLY GRATED

4-6 TABLESPOONS OLIVE OIL

SALT

TO SERVE

FRESHLY GRATED Parmesan CHEESE

VIRGIN OLIVE OIL

Cook the dried beans in boiling water for 10 minutes, cover, reduce the heat and simmer for 30 minutes. Drain, reserving the water. Measure the water and make up to 6 cups. Heat the oil in a saucepan, add the leeks and cook, stirring occasionally, until softened. Stir in the carrots and pumpkin and cook for 2-3 minutes before stirring in the soissons or cannellini beans and reserved cooking liquid. Cover and simmer gently for 45 minutes.

Add the remaining vegetables and pasta, season and cook gently for a further 15 minutes until tender.

Meanwhile, make the pistou; tear the basil leaves and put them in a mortar. Add the garlic and a pinch of salt and pound to a paste using a pestle. Add half the cheese and pound together. Mix with a little oil to moisten. Continue adding cheese and oil until well and evenly mixed. Spoon the pistou into a tureen, pour over the soup, cover and keep warm for 5 minutes. Serve with more Parmesan and olive oil.

Serves 4-6

AVGOLEMONO SOUP

The combination of eggs and lemon juice that is used as a thickener, known as Avgolemono, is the favorite Greek way of flavoring and thickening liquids at the same time. The liquid may be a sauce to accompany a pilaf or stuffed vine leaves, a casserole or, as here, a light fresh soup. Containing few ingredients, the quality of the soup rests mainly on the stock, which in coastal areas would be fish stock, while inland it would be chicken or meat. A few small pieces of fish, chicken or meat may be added and more or less rice or eggs used, depending on the thickness and type of soup required.

5 CUPS GOOD FISH OR CHICKEN STOCK

¼ CUP LONG GRAIN RICE

3 TABLESPOONS FINELY CHOPPED PARSLEY

2 OR 3 EGGS

6 TABLESPOONS LEMON JUICE

SALT AND PEPPER

Bring the stock to a boil, add the rice, cover and simmer for 15 minutes, or until the rice is tender. Add the parsley and season to taste.

Beat the eggs with the lemon juice, then whisk in a little of the hot stock. Very slowly pour the egg mixture into the saucepan, stirring constantly over a very low heat; the soup must not boil, otherwise it will curdle. Serve immediately.

Serves 4

TURKISH WALNUT SOUP

*This inspired combination of walnuts and orange is based
on a soup that I ate one day near Izmir. It was served in
large, chunky bowls in a simple country restaurant, more
like a private home than a commercial establishment. With
the soup came a plate piled high with hunks of brown bread,
warm from the oven, and a dish of pale, fresh unsalted
butter – a veritable feast. In a quest to find the secret of its
beauty, one of my companions enquired about the recipe,
but his Turkish could not cope with the heavy dialect of the
cook. However, I have subsequently discovered that plump,
fresh nuts are essential for a good soup.*

1½ CUPS SHELLED WALNUTS

1 TABLESPOON OLIVE OIL

4 SHALLOTS, CHOPPED

2 CLOVES OF GARLIC, CRUSHED

GOOD PINCH OF GROUND CINNAMON

GRATED RIND OF 1 ORANGE

JUICE OF 2 ORANGES

5 CUPS CHICKEN OR VEGETABLE STOCK

½ TABLESPOON WALNUT OIL

½ CUP GREEK STRAINED EWES' MILK YOGURT

SALT AND PEPPER

TO GARNISH

CHOPPED CILANTRO OR PARSLEY

GRATED ORANGE RIND

CHOPPED WALNUTS

Place the walnuts under a preheated broiler until crisp, then
coarsely chop them.

Meanwhile, heat the olive oil in a saucepan, add the
shallots and cook, stirring occasionally, until softened but
not colored. Stir in the garlic, cook for 2 minutes and then
stir in the cinnamon for about 30 seconds. Add the walnuts,
orange rind and orange juice and boil for about 1 minute.

Tip the mixture into a blender or food processor, add a
ladleful of the stock and the walnut oil and mix to a thick
purée. Add a little more stock to thin the purée, then pour
back into the saucepan, stir in the remaining stock, season
and bring to a boil. Simmer for 5-10 minutes, stirring
occasionally.

Over a low heat, whisk in the yogurt and heat through
very gently; do not allow the soup to get too hot. Serve
garnished with chopped cilantro or parsley, grated orange
rind and chopped walnuts.

Serves 4

PUMPKIN SOUP

*Mantua is the home of quite a repertoire of renowned
pumpkin dishes, including a most delicious risotto, delicate
gnocchi and "tortelli di zucca," which is traditionally served
on Christmas Eve, as well as the best pumpkin soup I have
ever encountered. In fact, pumpkin is eaten and enjoyed to
such an extent in Mantua that it has become the town's
emblem. What makes the Mantuan recipes so special is the
particular type of pumpkin – the magnificent yellow-fleshed
"zucca gialla." The nearest equivalent is butternut squash.*

*The soup is emulated elsewhere with many versions
evolving. One that I highly recommend trying is flavored
with a smidgen of saffron, and it really does make an
extremely good soup. In the recipe below, milk can be
substituted for half the stock, but it should not be added
until the soup is reheated after puréeing.*

2 LB BUTTERNUT SQUASH OR PUMPKIN

2 TABLESPOONS OLIVE OIL

½ CUP PROSCIUTTO, CHOPPED

2 ONIONS, CHOPPED

2½ CUPS CHICKEN OR VEGETABLE STOCK

1 BAY LEAF

SPRIG OF THYME

SALT AND PEPPER

BASIL LEAVES TO GARNISH

CROUTONS TO SERVE (SEE BROILED MEDITERRANEAN
VEGETABLE SOUP, PAGE 16)

Discard the seeds and stringy parts of the squash or
pumpkin, cut the flesh from the skin and chop it.

Heat the oil in a large saucepan, add the prosciutto and
onions and cook, stirring occasionally, until the onions are
soft but not colored. Stir in the squash or pumpkin for a few
seconds, then add the stock, bay leaf and thyme. Bring to a
boil, then simmer for 30 minutes until the squash or
pumpkin is very tender.

Discard the herbs and purée the soup in a blender or food
processor or pass it through a strainer. Return to the
saucepan. Add the seasoning and reheat gently. Serve the
soup with basil leaves sprinkled over and accompanied by
the croutons.

Serves 4

*Top: Turkish Walnut Soup
Bottom: Pumpkin Soup*

FISH SOUP

To choose one specific type of fish soup or stew recipe was an impossible task, as a whole chapter could be devoted to authentic Mediterranean fish soups, let alone all the personal variations. Bouillabaisse had to be omitted because it needs fish only available from the Mediterranean. In the end I opted for a hybrid that includes the features I particularly like, such as a mixture of seafish and shellfish, whole pieces of fish, a garlicky aïoli thickening, and a crisp croûtes topping spread with "hot" aïoli (definitely a main course soup), and have left others to make what adjustments they like. The most important principle is to use the freshest fish available and cook each type for its correct time.

3½-4 LB MIXED FISH WITH BONE, SUCH AS JOHN DORY,
GURNARD OR RED MULLET, SEA BREAM, MONKFISH, MUSSELS
AND UNCOOKED LARGE SHRIMP

EXTRA FISH HEADS AND BONES FOR THE STOCK

I CARROT, HALVED

I ONION, HALVED

BOUQUET GARNI OF I BAY LEAF, SEVERAL SPRIGS OF PARSLEY, 2 SPRIGS OF THYME
AND 3 SPRIGS OF FENNEL

¾ CUP MEDIUM-BODIED DRY WHITE WINE

7½ CUPS WATER

3 TABLESPOONS OLIVE OIL

2 LEEKS, THINLY SLICED

2 CLOVES OF GARLIC, CRUSHED

2 SUN-RIPENED EXTRA LARGE TOMATOES, SKINNED, DESEEDED AND CHOPPED

PINCH OF SAFFRON THREADS, TOASTED AND CRUSHED

½ SWEET RED PEPPER, CHARRED, CORED AND DESEEDED

DOUBLE QUANTITY AIOLI (SEE PAGE 24)

PINCH OF CHILE POWDER

4 EGG YOLKS

SALT AND PEPPER

TO SERVE

I SMALL FRENCH BREAD, SLICED AND DRIED IN A WARM OVEN UNTIL CRISP

FRESHLY GRATED PARMESAN CHEESE

Trim and clean the fish, reserving the heads and trimmings. Cut the fish into large chunks; remove the legs and any eggs from the shrimp. Scrub and debeard the mussel shells.

Put all the fish bones, heads and trimmings into a large saucepan with the carrot, onion, bouquet garni, wine and water. Bring slowly to a boil, skim off the scum from the surface and simmer for 25 minutes. Strain through a strainer lined with cheesecloth, pressing down well on the contents of the strainer.

Heat the oil in a large saucepan, add the leeks and garlic and cook, stirring occasionally, until softened but not colored. Stir in the tomatoes and saffron and bring to a boil. Simmer for 2-3 minutes, then pour in the fish stock and return to a boil. Lower the heat and add the fish, except for the shrimp and mussels. Poach for about 5 minutes before adding the mussels and shrimp and cooking for a further 5 minutes – take care not to overcook the fish.

Meanwhile, crush the red pepper in a mortar or a bowl and mix in half the Aïoli with a pestle or the end of a rolling pin. Add chile powder to taste. Spoon into a small serving bowl. Beat the egg yolks into the remaining Aïoli.

Using a slotted spoon, transfer the fish and shellfish to a large warm tureen; you can remove some or all of the skin and bones, if you like. Discard any mussels which have not opened. Cover and keep warm.

Stir a ladleful of the liquid into the Aïoli and egg yolk mixture. Lower the heat beneath the pan, then stir the Aïoli liquid into the pan. Heat gently, stirring constantly, until it begins to thicken; do not allow to boil. Adjust the seasoning to taste then pour over the fish. Spoon a few pieces of fish into each soup bowl, pour over a good ladle of soup, and serve with the French bread, red pepper sauce and Parmesan cheese so each person can spread sauce on the bread, place it on the soup and sprinkle over some Parmesan.
Serves 6

WHITE BEAN SOUP WITH GARLIC SAUCE

More or less identical soups based on dried white beans are popular in Italy, particularly Tuscany, as well as in Greece and Turkey.

6 TABLESPOONS OLIVE OIL

2 CLOVES OF GARLIC, CRUSHED

1 BAY LEAF

LEAVES FROM 2 SPRIGS OF THYME AND 2 SPRIGS OF OREGANO

1 SAGE LEAF, CHOPPED

2 CUPS CANNELLINI OR BORLOTTI BEANS, SOAKED OVERNIGHT
AND DRAINED

7½ CUPS BOILING WATER

1 LARGE ONION, CHOPPED

2 CARROTS, CHOPPED

1 BUNCH OF CELERY, CHOPPED

SALT AND PEPPER

FINELY CHOPPED PARSLEY TO GARNISH

SAUCE

3 EGG YOLKS

4 TABLESPOONS LEMON JUICE

3 CLOVES OF GARLIC, CRUSHED

¾ CUP UNSALTED BUTTER, MELTED UNTIL JUST BUBBLING

SALT AND PEPPER

Heat 4 tablespoons of the oil in a large heavy saucepan, add the garlic, herbs and beans and cook, stirring frequently, for about 5 minutes. Add the boiling water and simmer until the beans are tender, about 1 hour, depending on their age; add a little more water during cooking, if necessary.

Meanwhile, heat the remaining oil in an earthenware dish or frying pan, add the onion, carrots and celery, cover tightly and cook over a low heat, stirring occasionally, until soft, about 20 minutes.

Stir the vegetables into the beans and purée half the mixture in a blender or food processor. Return the purée to the remaining half, season and reheat gently.

To make the sauce, mix the egg yolks, lemon juice, garlic and seasoning in a blender. With the motor running, slowly add the melted butter and continue mixing for a few minutes to make a thick, creamy sauce. Transfer to a warm bowl.

To serve, pour the soup into individual bowls. Add a spoonful of the sauce to each and sprinkle with finely chopped parsley.

Serves 4

HARIRA

Spicy colorful Harira is a popular Moroccan dish.

½ LB LEAN LAMB, CUBED

2 TABLESPOONS OLIVE OIL

1 ONION, CHOPPED

½ CUP CHICK PEAS, SOAKED OVERNIGHT AND DRAINED

6 CUPS WATER

½ CUP RED LENTILS

3-4 TOMATOES, SKINNED, DESEEDED AND CHOPPED

1 TABLESPOON TOMATO PASTE

1 TEASPOON GROUND CINNAMON

1 SWEET RED PEPPER, CORED, DESEEDED AND CHOPPED

¼ CUP LONG-GRAIN RICE

BUNCH OF CILANTRO, CHOPPED

SALT AND PEPPER

Fry the lamb in the oil in a large saucepan until an even light brown. Stir in the onion and cook gently until softened. Add the chick peas and water, bring to a boil, cover and simmer for 1 hour, or until the chick peas are almost tender.

Add the lentils, tomatoes, tomato paste, cinnamon and red pepper and simmer for about 15 minutes. Add the rice, bring to a boil; simmer for further 15 minutes, until rice and lentils are tender. Stir in the cilantro and seasoning.

Serves 6

ANCHOÏADE

Serve Anchoïade as a dip for crudités, or spread on croûtes.

2 CLOVES OF GARLIC, CHOPPED

20 ANCHOVY FILLETS, RINSED IF NECESSARY

APPROXIMATELY 1½ TABLESPOONS TORN BASIL

5 TABLESPOONS VIRGIN OLIVE OIL

2-3 TEASPOONS RED WINE VINEGAR

2 TEASPOONS TOMATO PASTE, PREFERABLY SUN-DRIED (OPTIONAL)

PEPPER

Crush the garlic using a pestle and mortar, pound in the anchovies. Add the basil. Gradually pour in the oil in a slow trickle, pounding constantly, then the vinegar and paste, if using. Season. Keep in a covered glass jar in the refrigerator. Stir and adjust level of vinegar and basil before serving.

Serves 4

PESTO

Pesto is made all over Italy, but its "home" is Liguria, where, in the mild climate, a special variety of small-leaved, richly flavored basil thrives. The use of Pecorino Sardo, a Sardinian cheese, is a reminder that Genoa was part of the Sardinian kingdom until 1861. Using the traditional pestle and mortar produces Pesto with the best flavor and texture, but it is a little laborious. For many people, the speed and ease of using a blender outweighs the loss in quality, but for me this loss is too great and a mezzaluna produces a far more acceptable result. It is worth making a lot of Pesto when basil is in season. Either pack it into small, airtight jars and refrigerate (allow it to come to room temperature before using), or freeze it in ice cube trays and keep the cubes in a plastic bag ready for thawing individually in the refrigerator as required. When making Pesto purposely for freezing, I prefer not to add the cheese until it has thawed for use. The classic way of using Pesto is with trenette, the local Ligurian fettuccine, but there are innumerable other uses for it — spooned on to sliced tomatoes, served with plainly cooked meats, poultry and fish, added to sauces, casseroles and soups, as a filling for rolled fish fillets, or mixed with soft cheese and slipped between the skin and flesh of chicken portions.

1½ CUPS FRESH BASIL LEAVES

1-2 CLOVES OF GARLIC

2 TABLESPOONS PINE NUTS, LIGHTLY TOASTED

2 TABLESPOONS PARMESAN CHEESE, FRESHLY GRATED

1 TABLESPOON FRESHLY GRATED PECORINO SARDO CHEESE

APPROXIMATELY ½ CUP VIRGIN OLIVE OIL

SALT AND PEPPER

Put the basil, garlic, pine nuts and a pinch of salt in a mortar and grind with a pestle until a paste forms. Alternatively, chop with a mezzaluna. Add the cheeses and mix in well.

Slowly pour in the oil, stirring vigorously with a wooden spoon. Add black pepper to taste, if you like.

Pesto can be kept in a tightly covered jar in the refrigerator for up to one week.
Serves 4

Clockwise from bottom left: Pesto, Aïoli, Tapenade, Skorthalia, Toulouse Walnut Sauce, Anchoïade, Salmoriglio, Salsa Verde; Center: Sun-dried tomatoes

TAPENADE

Tapenade comes from "tapeno," the old Provençal word for caper, traditionally an important ingredient. Nowadays this is less so and capers are sometimes left out altogether.

1½ CUPS NOYONS BLACK OLIVES, PITTED

⅓ CUP CAPERS

4 ANCHOVY FILLETS, RINSED IF NECESSARY

1-2 CLOVES OF GARLIC, CRUSHED

1 TABLESPOON DIJON MUSTARD

½ CUP OLIVE OIL

1 TEASPOON CRUMBLED THYME

LEMON JUICE TO TASTE

PEPPER

Pound the olives, capers, anchovies, garlic and mustard together in a mortar to make a paste. Work in the oil a drop at a time, then add a little more quickly. Mix in the thyme, lemon juice and plenty of black pepper. Adjust the consistency (it should be a thick, spreadable paste) and pungency if necessary, adding more oil to mellow it. Tapenade can be kept in a tightly covered jar in the refrigerator for several weeks. Serve at room temperature.
Serves 4

SKORTHALIA

This pungent, Greek garlic sauce may be thickened with potato, bread or nuts, principally walnuts or almonds, and is served with poultry, fish (especially salt cod), broiled meats, vegetables, hard-boiled eggs and on bread.

4 SLICES OF WHITE BREAD, CRUSTS REMOVED, CRUMBLED

ABOUT 6 CLOVES OF GARLIC, CRUSHED

½ CUP OLIVE OIL

3 TABLESPOONS LEMON JUICE

SALT AND PEPPER

Soak the bread in water, then squeeze it dry. Pound the garlic with a pinch of salt in a mortar with a pestle. Pound in the bread, then add the oil, a drop at a time at first, increasing the rate as the mixture begins to form a sauce, mixing all the time. Add lemon juice and pepper to taste.
Serves 4

SALMORIGLIO

Throughout Sicily, Salmoriglio is brushed on fish threaded on skewers before being broiled, then served separately with the fish. Sicilians believe the only way to make a really good Salmoriglio is to add seawater; in my kitchen, I've made the nearest replica I can by seasoning with sea salt.

I TABLESPOON FINELY CHOPPED PARSLEY

1½ TEASPOONS CHOPPED OREGANO

APPROXIMATELY I TEASPOON FINELY CHOPPED ROSEMARY

I CLOVE OF GARLIC, CRUSHED

¾ CUP VIRGIN OLIVE OIL, WARMED SLIGHTLY

3 TABLESPOONS HOT WATER

ABOUT 4 TABLESPOONS LEMON JUICE

SEA SALT AND PEPPER

Pound together herbs, garlic and a pinch of salt in a mortar and pestle. Pour oil into a warmed bowl, then, using a fork, gradually whisk in the hot water then the lemon juice to make a thick, creamy sauce. Add herb mixture and pepper to taste, then place bowl over a saucepan of hot water for 5 minutes, whisking frequently. Serve in a warm gravy boat.
Serves 6

SALSA VERDE

This sauce is traditionally served with "bollito misto," a north Italian dish of mixed boiled meats and poultry.

2 SLICES OF WHITE BREAD, CRUSTS REMOVED, SOAKED IN WHITE WINE VINEGAR

I HARD-BOILED EGG, CHOPPED

3 ANCHOVY FILLETS, RINSED IF NECESSARY

LEAVES FROM A GOOD HANDFUL OF PARSLEY

I DRIED RED CHILE, CRUSHED

I TABLESPOON BALSAMIC VINEGAR

I TABLESPOON WHITE WINE VINEGAR

APPROXIMATELY 1¼ CUPS OLIVE OIL

2 CLOVES OF GARLIC, HALVED LENGTHWAYS

Squeeze the bread dry and pass through a strainer, with the egg and the anchovies, into a mortar. Pound in the parsley and chile, mix in the vinegars. Gradually beat in the oil using a fork or wire whisk. Add the garlic, cover and leave in the refrigerator for I day. Remove the garlic before serving.
Serves 6-8

AÏOLI AND AL-I-OLI

Aïoli is a Provençal sauce, which nowadays has come to be no more than mayonnaise with a garlic purée base, although originally it was based on bread crumbs. True Catalan Al-i-oli, however, should be made from just garlic ("al") and ("i") oil ("oli"), so it is white and shiny with a pronounced garlic flavor. Without eggs, it is trickier to make than Aïoli because the emulsion does not form readily and is less stable. Use a mild, sweet, clean-tasting olive oil and plump, crisp garlic that is as fresh as possible. As when making mayonnaise, all the ingredients must be at room temperature. Both sauces should be thicker than mayonnaise and, traditionally, are quite dense. Using a food processor or blender will alter this characteristic, as they incorporate air, thus changing their qualities. Aïoli and Al-i-oli have innumerable uses – served with broiled poultry, fish, meats and rabbit, with vegetables and eggs and spread on bread. Aïoli can also be used to thicken and flavor many recipes, such as seafood, noodle and rice dishes, soups and casseroles.

Aïoli

6-12 CLOVES OF GARLIC, CHOPPED

2 EGG YOLKS

½-I TEASPOON DIJON MUSTARD (OPTIONAL)

APPROXIMATELY 1¼ CUPS OLIVE OIL

1½-2 TABLESPOONS LEMON JUICE, WHITE WINE VINEGAR OR

A COMBINATION OF THE TWO

SALT AND PEPPER

Crush the garlic with a pinch of salt in a mortar using a pestle until mixed to a smooth paste, then work in the egg yolks, and mustard if using. Add the oil, a few drops at a time, while stirring slowly, evenly and constantly in the same direction. Once half the oil has been incorporated, add half the lemon juice, white wine vinegar or combination, adding the remainder when all the oil has been incorporated.

Al-i-oli – omit the egg yolks, mustard and pepper, and – according to some sources – the lemon juice or vinegar. Reduce the quantity of oil to about I cup and stop adding it when an emulsion forms – to continue will cause the emulsion to "break." Serve immediately.

Al-i-oli and Aïoli with Roasted Garlic – use more cloves of roasted garlic for a sweeter, milder flavor.
Serves 4

NUT SAUCES

In the Middle East and Turkey, all nut sauces tend to go under the name of tarator, although they may taste quite different. Traditionally, nut sauces are made using a pestle and mortar, but you could add the whole nuts to a small blender, and add the soaked bread and garlic. Mix together and slowly pour in the oil, mixing at slow speed and increasing the flow as the sauce thickens. Add lemon juice, water and seasoning as required. Serve at room temperature or lightly chilled, with fish, chicken, meats and vegetables.

LEBANESE TARATOR WITH PINE NUTS

1½ SLICES OF COUNTRY BREAD (SEE PAGE 113), CRUSTS REMOVED, TORN

1-2 CLOVES OF GARLIC, CRUSHED

2 CUPS PINE NUTS, CHOPPED

1 CUP OLIVE OIL

2-3 TABLESPOONS LEMON JUICE

SALT AND WHITE PEPPER

Soak the bread in a little water. Pound the garlic with a little salt in a mortar, then add and pound the nuts. Squeeze the bread dry, then work it into the sauce. Gradually mix in the oil, followed by lemon juice to taste and enough of the water to give a smooth light cream. Season to taste.
Serves 4

TURKISH TARATOR WITH HAZELNUTS, OR WALNUTS

1 SLICE OF COUNTRY BREAD (SEE PAGE 113), CRUSTS REMOVED

1 PLUMP CLOVE OF GARLIC, CRUSHED

1 CUP HAZELNUTS OR WALNUTS, AS FRESH AS POSSIBLE, CHOPPED

½ CUP CHICKEN STOCK

APPROXIMATELY 2 TABLESPOONS LEMON JUICE

SALT AND PEPPER

Soak the bread in a little water. Pound the garlic with a little salt in a mortar. Add and pound the hazelnuts or walnuts. Squeeze the bread dry and work it into the sauce, followed by the chicken stock, lemon juice and pepper to taste.
Serves 4

TARATOR WITH TAHINI

2 CLOVES OF GARLIC

⅓ CUP TAHINI

¼ TO ½ CUP WATER

APPROXIMATELY ½ CUP LEMON JUICE

SALT AND PEPPER

Crush the garlic with pinch of salt, then beat in the tahini using a wooden spoon. Alternately beat in a little water and lemon juice; the former thickens the sauce, the latter thins it. Incorporate all of the lemon juice and sufficient water to give a sauce of the desired consistency, depending on its use. Season with salt and pepper.
Serves 4

Variation
Tarator with Tahini and Parsley – add a handful of finely chopped parsley after all the lemon juice and about half of the water have been added. Do not add more water unless the mixture is too thick. Serve as a dip or an accompaniment to simple fish dishes.

TOULOUSE WALNUT SAUCE (AILLADE)

1 CUP WALNUTS, AS FRESH AS POSSIBLE

2 CLOVES OF GARLIC, CRUSHED

⅓ CUP LIGHT OLIVE OIL

⅓ CUP WALNUT OIL

LEMON JUICE

2 TABLESPOONS WATER

CHOPPED PARSLEY OR CHIVES

SALT AND PEPPER

Lightly toast the walnuts, let cool slightly then chop roughly. Pound the garlic with a little salt in a mortar, then add and pound the walnuts. Gradually mix in the oils, followed by lemon juice to taste and enough of the water to give a smooth light cream. Season to taste. Just before serving, sprinkle with parsley or chives.
Serves 6

Tapas, Antipasti & Mezzes

Mediterraneans eat late, especially in the evening, so these tapas, antipasti and mezzes constitute a civilized way of whiling away the time before dinner and staving off the hunger pangs as well – although, conversely, their traditional function was to whet the appetite. One of the best-loved features of Mediterranean life is this practice of casually tasting a morsel from here and another from there – choosing from an appetizing and varied selection of individual dishes, while chatting, enjoying a drink (where it is allowed) or just watching the world go by.

MARINATED ZUCCHINI

Marinating foods, "a scapece," is a very old method of preservation. Some say the name is derived from that of Apicius, the author of the earliest known cook book, De Re Coquinaria. Nowadays, the method is used simply as another way of preparing foods, usually fish and vegetables. Here, the combination of zucchini, lemon and herbs makes a light and refreshing dish.

4-5 ZUCCHINI, CUT INTO ¼ INCH SLICES

OLIVE OIL

LEAVES FROM A BUNCH OF BASIL

3 TABLESPOONS MINT LEAVES

2 SMALL CLOVES OF GARLIC, FINELY CHOPPED

2 TABLESPOONS LEMON JUICE

SALT AND PEPPER

Layer the zucchini slices and salt in a colander and leave for 30 minutes. Rinse the zucchini well and pat dry.

Heat a ¼ inch layer of oil in a large frying pan, add the zucchini slices in batches so they are not crowded and cook for about 3 minutes each side until golden. Using a slotted spoon, transfer to paper towels to drain.

Arrange the zucchini slices on a plate, tucking basil and mint leaves between them. Sprinkle with the garlic, lemon juice and seasonings and leave for at least 2 hours, preferably overnight, in the refrigerator, but return to room temperature about 30 minutes before serving.
Serves 4

FAVA BEANS WITH HAM

I have sampled innumerable variations on the theme of fava beans and ham. Some have been more or less just the beans and ham; at Rondena, in Andalusia, the cooking juices were thickened with bread crumbs and chopped hard-boiled egg was added, whereas in the colder climate of the Asturias, carrots and potatoes padded out the dish. However, this particularly colorful and tasty version is my favorite.

2 TABLESPOONS OLIVE OIL

4 LARGE SCALLIONS, FINELY CHOPPED

I SWEET RED PEPPER, CORED, DESEEDED AND DICED

50 G (2 OZ) SERRANO HAM, DICED

I½ CUPS SHELLED FAVA BEANS

APPROXIMATELY ¾ CUP MEDIUM-BODIED DRY

WHITE WINE

SALT AND PEPPER

Heat the oil in a saucepan and add the scallions, red pepper and ham and cook for 3 minutes. Stir in the beans for I minute, then add sufficient wine to cover the vegetables. Bring quickly to a boil, cover the pan and simmer gently until the beans are tender, about 15-20 minutes. Uncover and boil off excess liquid, if necessary. Add pepper and salt if necessary – this will depend on the saltiness of the ham. Cool slightly before serving.
Serves 4

Variation

Greek Fava Beans with Dill – gently cook 2 bunches of sliced, plump scallions in 3 tablespoons olive oil in a heavy pan, until soft. Stir in I½ cups shelled fresh young fava beans and cook gently for 2-3 minutes. Add 2-3 tablespoons chopped dill, salt and pepper and sufficient water to just cover the beans. Cover and cook gently until the beans are tender. Serve with Greek ewes' milk yogurt.

Clockwise from top right: Marinated Zucchini, Crostini, Tortilla with Sweet Red Pepper, Marinated Olives and Fava Beans with Ham

MARINATED OLIVES

With about 190 million olive trees in Spain it is no surprise that olives appear at virtually every tapas bar and almost automatically accompany every alcoholic drink. Marinating olives with herbs and spices gives additional distinction and is a way for a bar to personalize the olives it serves.

I LB GREEN OR BLACK OLIVES

I FRESH RED CHILE, DESEEDED AND CHOPPED

4 CLOVES OF GARLIC, CRUSHED

I SPRIG OF OREGANO

I SPRIG OF THYME

I TEASPOON FINELY CHOPPED ROSEMARY

2 BAY LEAVES

I TEASPOON FENNEL SEEDS, BRUISED

I TEASPOON ROASTED AND FINELY CRUSHED CUMIN SEEDS

OLIVE OIL TO COVER

Using a small sharp knife make a lengthways slit through to the stone of each olive. Put the olives into a bowl and stir in the chile, garlic, oregano, thyme, rosemary, bay leaves, fennel seeds and cumin.

Pack the olive mixture into a screw-top jar and cover with olive oil. Close the jar and leave the olives for at least 3 days, shaking jar occasionally, before using. If stored in a cool, dark place the olives will keep for several months.
Serves 4

CROSTINI

Crostini are simply slices of bread toasted in the oven, topped with something savory and served warm. They may be first rubbed with garlic then trickled with good olive oil. The bread is very important – the edges should be firm and crusty, while the middle should have a chewy texture that is able to absorb any juices that might seep from the topping. Good examples are Italian and French country bread and ciabatta.

Cut the bread into ½ inch thick slices then bake in a single layer on a baking pan in a preheated oven, 400°F, until lightly browned, turning once, for 5-10 minutes.
Serves 4

CROSTINI TOPPINGS

• tapenade, anchoïade, pesto, perhaps topped with a slice of tomato.

• tapenade, anchoïade, pesto, topped with a slice of mozzarella cheese and chopped or sliced tomato; pop back into the oven for a few minutes.

• soft goats' cheese mixed with chopped basil or tarragon or thyme, topped with sliced sun-dried tomatoes.

• sun-dried tomato paste sprinkled with Pecorino and broiled.

• cold, thick peperonata, ratatouille, caponata.

• grated Scamorza cheese (smoked mozzarella), sprinkled with a little finely chopped sage, seasoned and trickled with olive oil; broil until the cheese melts.

• sliced mozzarella cheese topped with a slice of eggplant, sprinkled with grated mozzarella and chopped parsley and basil; then broiled until the cheese has melted and turned golden.

• Gorgonzola mashed with a little cream, topped with chopped walnuts; then popped under a hot broiler.

• warm asparagus spears sprinkled with lemon juice on anchoïade, placed briefly under the broiler. Finish with finely chopped hard-boiled egg, if you like.

• chicken livers or wild, shiitake or oyster mushrooms sautéed in olive oil with finely chopped red onion and garlic; mash with a little chopped sage and seasoning.

• spread with ¾ cup pitted black, oil-packed olives coarsely puréed with ½ cup olive oil, ½ cup oil-packed sun-dried tomatoes, 2 teaspoons Dijon mustard, 2 teaspoons lemon juice and pepper; garnish with basil or parsley.

• 4-5 medium sun-ripened tomatoes, skinned, deseeded and chopped, mixed with the chopped leaves of a bunch of basil, 4 finely chopped cloves of garlic and 4 tablespoons virgin olive oil. Leave for 30 minutes, then stir in ¾ cup black oil-packed olives, pitted and chopped. Add pepper to taste. Garnish with strips of anchovy fillet and basil sprigs.

SPINACH-STUFFED MUSHROOMS

On most mornings when we were staying in a "mas," a stone farmhouse, nestled secretively in the hills behind Aix-en-Provence, we would be at the daily markets in the town soon after they opened at 8.00 am, so that we could take our pick of the choicest finds – fist-size Cavaillon melons, dried lime blossom ("tilleul"), for delicate tea and poached chicken, sweet peaches and nectarines, black figs with their scarlet interiors, large zucchini blossoms, small peppers and eggplants and whatever wild mushrooms resulted from early morning walks through the countryside. Back at the farmhouse we often turned the vegetables and zucchini flowers into a selection of Provençal petits farcis. This is the recipe we used for the mushrooms.

¾ LB SPINACH, STALKS REMOVED

I LB MEDIUM CAP MUSHROOMS

2 TABLESPOONS OLIVE OIL, PLUS EXTRA FOR BRUSHING

2 TABLESPOONS BACON, CHOPPED

I SMALL SHALLOT, FINELY CHOPPED

I CLOVE OF GARLIC, FINELY CHOPPED

¼ CUP SOFT GOATS' CHEESE

¼ CUP PARMESAN CHEESE, FRESHLY GRATED

2 TABLESPOONS FRESH BREAD CRUMBS

SALT AND PEPPER

Wash the spinach but do not dry it. Put it into a saucepan and cook, stirring occasionally, until wilted and no liquid is visible. Tip into a colander and squeeze out as much liquid as possible. Chop finely. Snap the stalks from the mushrooms and chop them finely.

Heat the oil in a frying pan, add the bacon, shallot, garlic and mushroom stalks and cook, stirring occasionally, for about 5 minutes. Stir in the spinach. Soon afterwards, remove the pan from the heat and stir in the goats' cheese, and salt and pepper.

Brush the mushroom caps lightly with oil and place them, gills uppermost, in a single layer in an oiled shallow baking dish. Divide the spinach mixture evenly between the mushrooms. Mix together the Parmesan cheese and bread crumbs, sprinkle over the mushrooms and bake in a preheated oven, 375°F, for about 20 minutes, until the mushrooms are tender. Serve warm.

Serves 4

MUSHROOMS WITH GARLIC AND PARSLEY

To be truly authentic wild mushrooms should be used, the exact type changing with the time of year, but I think oyster mushrooms are perfectly acceptable to use, or failing those, cremini mushrooms. The recipe is more usually made without the pine nuts, but I like the contrasting texture and flavor they bring.

3 TABLESPOONS OLIVE OIL

2 CLOVES OF GARLIC, FINELY CHOPPED

I LB OYSTER MUSHROOMS, CUT INTO LARGE PIECES

4 TABLESPOONS FINO SHERRY

½ CUP PINE NUTS

SQUEEZE OF LEMON JUICE

2 TABLESPOONS CHOPPED PARSLEY

SALT AND PEPPER

Heat the oil in a large frying pan and add the garlic. Cook over a fairly high heat until it is just beginning to brown, about 3 minutes.

Stir in the mushrooms, sherry and pine nuts and continue to cook until the mushroom juices have almost evaporated. Add lemon juice and salt and pepper to taste, stir in the parsley and serve.

Serves 4

Left: Spinach-stuffed Mushrooms
Right: Mushrooms with Garlic and Parsley

TORTILLA WITH SWEET RED PEPPER

The "classic" tortilla contains only potatoes and, perhaps, onion, but I prefer to add some other flavorings as well, such as sweet red pepper and chorizo. Another favorite that I make when fleshy artichokes are around is tortilla with artichoke and serrano ham.

6 TABLESPOONS OLIVE OIL

3 MEDIUM POTATOES, DICED

1 SPANISH ONION, CHOPPED

1 LARGE SWEET RED PEPPER, CORED, DESEEDED AND CHOPPED

5 EGGS

½ CUP CHORIZO, CHOPPED

SALT AND PEPPER

Heat the oil in a large, heavy frying pan, preferably non-stick. Season the potatoes and onion and add to the pan with the red pepper. Cook, covered, over a low heat until soft but not brown, about 20 minutes, stirring gently occasionally to prevent sticking. Drain off and reserve the oil.

In a small bowl, lightly beat the eggs with a little seasoning. Mix in the potatoes, onions, red pepper and chorizo and leave for 10 minutes.

Wipe the pan with paper towels and add enough of the reserved oil to cover the base with a thin film. Add the egg mixture, spreading it evenly in the pan. Cook over a moderate heat, shaking the pan occasionally, until the underside is set and beginning to brown.

Cover the pan with a large plate and hold it in place with one hand. Quickly invert the pan so the omelet falls on to the plate. Return the pan to the heat, add a little more oil and slide the omelet back into the pan, with the cooked side uppermost. Continue to cook until lightly browned underneath. Slide on to a serving plate and serve warm or at room temperature.
Serves 4 as a main course, or 8 for tapa

BLACK FIGS WITH MASCARPONE AND PROSCIUTTO

This recipe takes the well-known and equally well-loved combination of figs and Parma ham one stage further.

3 PLUMP, RIPE BLACK FIGS, QUARTERED

⅔ CUP RICH FRENCH DRESSING (SEE PAGE 52)

12 THIN SLICES OF PARMA HAM

12 HEAPING TEASPOONS MASCARPONE CHEESE

MINT LEAVES TO GARNISH

Toss the figs in the French dressing. Lay out the slices of ham and fold the long sides in to the middle. Place a fig quarter and a teaspoon of cheese at the end of each slice, then roll up to enclose. Place seam-side down on a serving plate. Garnish with mint leaves.
Serves 4

SCALLOPS WITH DILL

12 SCALLOPS, SHELLED

½ CUCUMBER, PEELED AND HALVED LENGTHWAYS

8 TABLESPOONS LEMON JUICE

2 TABLESPOONS CHOPPED DILL

1 TABLESPOON CHOPPED MINT

1 TABLESPOON VIRGIN OLIVE OIL

SALT AND PEPPER

LEMON SLICES AND MINT LEAVES TO GARNISH

If necessary, remove and discard from the scallop bodies the white muscle opposite the corals. Separate the corals from the bodies, then slice the bodies in half horizontally. Season with pepper.

Scoop out and discard the seeds from the cucumber and cut the flesh into pieces about the same size as the scallops. Add to boiling salted water, boil for 1 minute and drain.

Thread scallops, cucumber and corals on skewers alternately, then lay in a shallow non-metallic dish. Mix together the lemon juice, herbs and oil, pour over the scallops and cucumber, turn to coat with the marinade and leave for about 1 hour. Transfer the skewers to a broiler rack and place under a preheated hot broiler for 8-10 minutes, brushing with the remaining marinade occasionally and turning halfway through. Serve with lemon and mint.
Serves 4 as a first course, 2 as a light main course

PICKLED TURNIPS

Pickled turnips are very popular in the Middle East. Large jars of them are prepared by many families and they are a common sight in shop and restaurant windows, for sale in the streets and at the table. Even so, I had not expected them to be particularly to my taste, and I was very pleasantly surprised when I took my first bite of the pretty pink vegetable – it had a delicate, sweet sharpness and light crispness that I instantly found most appealing.

¼ CUP COARSE SALT

2 CUPS WATER

I CUP WHITE WINE VINEGAR

2 LB SMALL TURNIPS, HALVED

I SMALL UNCOOKED BEET, PEELED AND SLICED

2-4 CLOVES OF GARLIC (OPTIONAL)

FEW CELERY LEAVES

Bring the salt and water to a boil over a low heat, stirring. Remove from the heat, add the vinegar and let cool.

Layer the turnips, beet slices, garlic, if using, and the celery leaves in a sterilized preserving jar. Pour the cooled brine over the vegetables to cover them completely. Slip a fine knife or skewer down the inside of the jar in several places to dislodge any air bubbles. Place a small saucer, or something similar that will fit inside the jar, on top of the turnips, with a weight on top if necessary. Close the jar tightly and leave on a sunny window sill, or any other warm place for about 2 weeks.

The pickled turnips will keep for 2-3 months in the refrigerator.

Serves 4

BROILED RADICCHIO

The most famous and best radicchio comes from Treviso, near Venice. It is a winter vegetable, cultivated under straw and as the heads grow through the straw, they look like red snowdrops. With spear-shaped, crisp leaves, radicchio di Treviso looks something like a small, red romaine lettuce and has a unique flavor. Unfortunately, it is hard, but not impossible, to find here; instead we usually have a variety recently developed by growers near Chioggia, south of Venice. It grows all year round, looks more like a round cabbage and tastes slightly more bitter. Nevertheless, I have never had any complaints when I have served these broiled heads with the savory, melting surprise that oozes from the center.

4 SMALL HEADS OF RADICCHIO

4 MINIATURE MOZZARELLA BALLS

(*BOCCONCINI*), DRAINED

4 SMALL ANCHOVY FILLETS, COARSELY CHOPPED

2 TEASPOONS FINELY CHOPPED PARSLEY

CRUSHED DRIED RED CHILE (OPTIONAL)

EXTRA-VIRGIN OLIVE OIL

PEPPER

LEMON WEDGES TO SERVE

Gently open out the leaves of each head of radicchio and place a ball of mozzarella in the center; remove I or 2 of the inner leaves, if necessary. Top with one quarter of the anchovy and parsley. Season with black pepper, and crushed chile, if liked, and trickle over a few drops of olive oil. Carefully close the leaves over the cheese and secure with wooden toothpicks.

Brush the radicchio with olive oil then cook under a preheated moderate broiler, turning occasionally, for about 8 minutes, until golden. Remove the toothpicks and serve immediately with lemon wedges.

Serves 4

Variation
Broiled Radicchio with Goats' Cheese – halve 2 small heads of radicchio lengthways and remove a few of the central leaves to form a hollow. Place, cut side up in a broiler pan. Place a slice of goats' cheese in each hollow, brush the leaves and cheese with olive oil then broil until the cheese is bubbling. Sprinkle with chopped thyme or torn basil leaves.

33

GNOCCHI

Gnocchi can be made from potatoes and flour, from pumpkin, a mixture of spinach and ricotta cheese, or from semolina (which, in reality are baked discs of polenta made with milk instead of water). The essence of all good gnocchi, no matter from what they are made, is their lightness. Gnocchi are usually simmered in water, then served simply with melted butter and grated Parmesan cheese or a sauce such as Gorgonzola or tomato. The ridges on gnocchi are not purely cosmetic; they make the cooking quicker and more even throughout and provide a surface for the sauce to cling to. Potato gnocchi are the most common type. The quantity of flour and egg will depend on the type and dryness of the potatoes.

4 MEDIUM, ALL-PURPOSE, FLOURY POTATOES

I EGG, BEATEN

PINCH OF GRATED NUTMEG (OPTIONAL)

JUST UNDER 1¾ CUPS ALL-PURPOSE FLOUR

SALT AND PEPPER

GORGONZOLA SAUCE OR PESTO (SEE PAGE 23) TO SERVE

Boil the potatoes in their skins until tender. Drain and, protecting your hand with a towel, peel the hot potatoes, then pass through a vegetable mill or strainer. Mix in the egg, nutmeg, if you like, seasonings, and about half of the flour. Gradually add more flour until the mixture is soft, smooth and slightly sticky. Shape into rolls about I inch in diameter, then cut into ¾ inch pieces.

To shape the gnocchi, hold a fork in one hand, take I piece of gnocchi in the other and press it lightly with the thumb of your other hand against the inner curve of the prongs. Then, with a quick downwards movement, flip it towards the ends of the prongs so the gnocchi is concave on the thumb side, convex and ridged on the other. Gently lower the gnocchi in batches into plenty of just simmering salted water and poach until they come to the surface. Leave for a few seconds, then transfer to a warmed serving dish and serve with Gorgonzola sauce or Pesto.

Serves 6-8

Variation
Spinach and Potato Gnocchi – mix ⅓ cup cooked and thoroughly drained spinach into the potatoes after straining them.

SPINACH AND RICOTTA GNOCCHI

The lightest, most tender and delicious gnocchi, these are my favorite. However, if due diligence is not paid to drying the spinach adequately, the gnocchi are liable to disintegrate when cooked. So be warned. Without flour, the gnocchi are very delicate and need careful handling, so you may prefer to incorporate a couple of spoonfuls.

2 LB FRESH SPINACH

APPROXIMATELY 2 TABLESPOONS ALL-PURPOSE FLOUR (OPTIONAL)

I LARGE EGG, BEATEN

I CUP FRESH RICOTTA CHEESE

½ CUP PARMESAN CHEESE, FRESHLY GRATED

PINCH OF FRESHLY GRATED NUTMEG

SEASONED ALL-PURPOSE FLOUR FOR COATING

SALT AND PEPPER

TO SERVE

MELTED UNSALTED BUTTER

FRESHLY GRATED PARMESAN CHEESE

Remove the stalks from the spinach, then wash but do not dry the leaves. Chop them and heat in a saucepan until they wilt and any visible liquid has disappeared. Tip into a strainer and squeeze out as much liquid as possible – this is very important. Return to the saucepan, add the flour, if using, and heat gently, stirring to complete the drying. Remove from the heat, beat in the egg and mix in the two cheeses, nutmeg and seasoning.

Break off small balls of the mixture and roll lightly in seasoned flour to coat lightly and evenly and form into gnocchi (see recipe left). Continue with the remaining mixture, then chill for about I hour.

Half fill a large frying pan with water, bring to simmering point then carefully lower in some of the spinach shapes, but do not crowd the pan. Poach until they rise to the surface. Using a slotted spoon, transfer to a warm plate. Cook the remaining shapes in the same way. Serve warm with melted butter trickled over and sprinkled with Parmesan cheese.

Serves 4

Left: Spinach and Ricotta Gnocchi
Right: Gnocchi

HUMMUS

I have been imprecise about quantities for this chick pea and sesame dip because people's tastes vary considerably, but the flavor of sesame should not overtake that of the chick peas. Egyptians flavor the purée with enough cumin so that it is apparent but not dominant. The traditional garnish is pomegranate seeds. Whole cooked chick peas are sometimes used instead, and ground cumin or chopped parsley sprinkled over the top with the paprika.

1 HEAPING CUP CHICK PEAS, SOAKED OVERNIGHT AND DRAINED

2-3 CLOVES OF GARLIC, CRUSHED

APPROXIMATELY 1 CUP LEMON JUICE

APPROXIMATELY 5 TABLESPOONS TAHINI

SALT

WARM PITA BREAD TO SERVE

TO GARNISH

OLIVE OIL

PAPRIKA

Cook the chick peas in plenty of boiling water until soft – 1-1½ hours depending on their quality and age. Drain and reserve the cooking liquid. Purée the chick peas in a blender or food processor with a little of the cooking liquid, then press the purée through a strainer to remove the skins.

Crush the garlic with a little salt and beat into the chick pea purée. Stir in the lemon juice and tahini alternately, tasting before it has all been added to get the right balance of flavors. Add a little more salt, if necessary, and more of the cooking liquid to make a soft, creamy consistency. Spoon the purée into a shallow dish, cover and leave in the refrigerator for several hours.

Return to room temperature a short while before serving so that the purée is not too cold. Create swirls in the surface with the back of a spoon then trickle olive oil into the whirls and sprinkle lightly with paprika. Serve with warm pita bread.

Serves 6

EGGPLANT DIP

I have eaten many mezzes but, without doubt, the best were the 25 that the ever-helpful team at the Dubai Hilton rustled up at a moment's notice for me to try. Their way with the eggplant dip, which I always follow now, was to leave some texture to it, rather than reducing the flesh to an homogenous purée, and not to dilute it with tahini or yogurt, as is sometimes the case.

APPROXIMATELY 1½ MEDIUM EGGPLANTS

APPROXIMATELY 4 TABLESPOONS FAIRLY MILD OLIVE OIL

APPROXIMATELY 3 TABLESPOONS LEMON JUICE

2 CLOVES OF GARLIC, VERY FINELY CHOPPED

½ SMALL MILD ONION, VERY FINELY CHOPPED

1½ TABLESPOONS VERY FINELY CHOPPED SWEET RED PEPPER

SALT AND PEPPER

WARM PITA BREAD TO SERVE

TO GARNISH

OLIVE OIL

CHOPPED PARSLEY

Broil the eggplants, turning frequently, until the skin is charred and blistered and the flesh feels soft when the eggplant is pressed. When cool enough to handle, remove and discard the stems and skin. Squeeze the flesh gently to expel surplus liquid.

Chop the eggplant flesh so that it still has some texture. Place in a bowl and pour in the oil. Mix in most of the lemon juice and stir in the garlic, onion, red pepper and salt and pepper. Taste and add more lemon juice, if necessary. Cover and leave in the refrigerator for several hours.

Return to room temperature a short while before serving so that the purée is not too cold. Spoon it into a flat dish and make a few swirls in the surface with the back of a spoon. Pour a thin trickle of olive oil into the whirls and garnish with chopped parsley. Serve with warm pita bread.

Serves 6

TABBOULEH

I have been told so many different things, all equally adamantly, about how Tabbouleh should be made — the length of time the burghul should be left to soak (the longer the soaking, the softer it will become; the fineness of the burghul also comes into play); what the proportion of burghul to parsley should be; whether mint should be included and, if so, how much; the amount of scallions, oil and lemon juice, whether tomatoes should be in the salad as well as on top, and so on. Thus I have concluded that the only right thing to do is to make it the way you like it. Then, at least you will be happy. However, there are two practical points you may find useful: if you chop the herbs in a food processor, use the pulse action to avoid turning them to sludge, and if incorporating tomatoes, do not do so too far in advance.

⅓ CUP BURGHUL

4 TABLESPOONS LEMON JUICE

4 TABLESPOONS OLIVE OIL

2 CUPS FLAT-LEAVED PARSLEY, FINELY CHOPPED

3-4 TABLESPOONS FINELY CHOPPED MINT (OPTIONAL)

5 SCALLIONS, FINELY CHOPPED

3 SUN-RIPENED TOMATOES, DESEEDED AND DICED

SALT AND PEPPER

INNER LEAVES OF CRISP LETTUCE TO SERVE

BLACK OLIVES TO GARNISH

Pour enough water over the burghul to cover it and leave for 15 minutes. Drain through a strainer then squeeze out the excess moisture. Tip into a bowl. Stir in the lemon juice and oil and salt and pepper. Leave until plump and tender.

Mix the herbs then stir into the burghul with the scallions and tomatoes. Adjust the seasoning and quantity of lemon juice, if necessary. Serve on a large flat serving dish lined with lettuce and garnish with black olives.

Serves 4

DOLMADES

Popular throughout the eastern Mediterranean, Dolmades (stuffed vine leaves) may be served hot or cold and may contain meat, or be meatless as in this recipe. Fresh leaves are sometimes available from Greek and Cypriot shops. If using leaves packed in brine, rinse them well, then blanch in boiling water for 3 minutes and drain well.

¼ CUP LONG-GRAIN RICE

½ CUP BOILING WATER

12 FRESH VINE LEAVES

1½ TABLESPOONS OLIVE OIL

1 SMALL ONION, CHOPPED

25 G (1 OZ) PINE NUTS

3 MEDIUM SUN-RIPENED TOMATOES, SKINNED, DESEEDED AND CHOPPED

1-2 TEASPOONS TOMATO PASTE

1 TABLESPOON CHOPPED PARSLEY

1 TABLESPOON CHOPPED MINT

¼ TEASPOON GROUND CINNAMON

3 CLOVES OF GARLIC, CRUSHED

2 TABLESPOONS LEMON JUICE

1 TABLESPOON CHOPPED OREGANO

SALT AND PEPPER

Cook rice in the boiling salted water in a covered pan for 12-15 minutes until tender and the liquid has been absorbed.

Meanwhile, blanch the vine leaves, in batches, in plenty of boiling water for 30 seconds, then turn them over. Drain in a colander, rinse under cold running water, then spread out each leaf, vein-side uppermost.

Heat the oil in a frying pan, add the onion and pine nuts and cook, stirring, until browned. Stir in the cooked rice, one third of the tomatoes, the tomato paste, parsley, mint, cinnamon and 2 garlic cloves for a couple of minutes. Stir in the lemon juice and seasoning, remove from the heat.

Place half the remaining tomatoes in a small flameproof casserole dish. Put a spoon of the rice mixture on to the stalk end of a vine leaf, fold the sides over the filling, then roll up the leaf and press into a sausage shape. Place, seam-side down, in the casserole dish. Repeat with the remaining rice mixture and leaves, packing them into the casserole dish. Put the remaining tomatoes, garlic and oregano on top, season and place a plate on top to prevent the vine leaves unrolling during cooking. Cover the casserole dish, cook gently for 2 hours. Serve with the juices spooned over.

Serves 6 as a first course, 4 as a main course

SIZZLING SHRIMP WITH GARLIC AND CHILE

The sound, as well as the smell, heralds the approach of a small cazuela of gambas al pil-pil, to use the onomatopoeic Spanish name. The generous amount of oil in which the shrimp are cooked should still be actively sizzling when they are served, so that they stay crisp and dry. Each dish is carried to the table covered by a piece of bread, which serves the dual roles of stopping the oil spitting and providing a "mop" for the flavorsome cooking juices.

½ CUP OLIVE OIL

4-5 CLOVES OF GARLIC, FINELY CRUSHED

I FRESH RED CHILE, DESEEDED AND CHOPPED

I LB RAW SHRIMP, PEELED

2-3 TABLESPOONS CHOPPED PARSLEY

SEA SALT

TO SERVE

LEMON WEDGES

4 SLICES OF COUNTRY BREAD (SEE PAGE 113)

Heat the oil in 4 individual flameproof earthenware dishes over a high heat. Add the garlic and chile, cook for 1-2 minutes, then add the shrimp and sea salt.

Cook briskly for 2-3 minutes, shaking the dishes frequently. Stir in the parsley and serve the shrimp at once accompanied by lemon wedges, and bread to mop up the juices.

Serves 4

MUSSELS WITH PROSCIUTTO

Although "cozze" is the correct name for mussels, do not be surprised if, when in Liguria and Venezia Giulia, a shellfish called "mitili" turns out to be mussels. The same applies to "muscol'" in the Marches (and possibly elsewhere), and "peoci" around Venice, from where this recipe comes.

2 LB MUSSELS, SCRUBBED AND DEBEARDED

2 SUN-RIPENED TOMATOES, SKINNED, DESEEDED AND

FINELY CHOPPED

4 TABLESPOONS FINELY CHOPPED PROSCIUTTO

2 TABLESPOONS FINELY CHOPPED PARSLEY

I CLOVE OF GARLIC, FINELY CHOPPED

PINCH OF PAPRIKA

APPROXIMATELY 2 TABLESPOONS DRY BREAD CRUMBS

2 TABLESPOONS VIRGIN OLIVE OIL

COOKING LIQUID (OPTIONAL)

4 CLOVES OF GARLIC, FINELY CHOPPED

½ TEASPOON CRUSHED DRIED RED PEPPER FLAKES

5 TABLESPOONS FINELY CHOPPED PARSLEY

5 TABLESPOONS VIRGIN OLIVE OIL

½ CUP MEDIUM-BODIED DRY WHITE WINE

If making the cooking liquid, cook the garlic, crushed red pepper flakes and parsley in the oil in a large saucepan over a medium heat until the garlic is fragrant. Add the wine and mussels, cover and cook for 4-5 minutes, shaking the pan occasionally, until the mussels open; discard any mussels that remain closed.

If not making the cooking liquid, simply cook the mussels in 4 tablespoons water in a saucepan.

Twist off the top shells, leaving the mussels in the lower shells. Place on a rack in a large baking dish.

In a small bowl, combine the tomatoes, prosciutto, parsley, garlic and paprika. Divide between the mussels. Top each with a pinch of bread crumbs, then trickle olive oil over them. Bake in a preheated oven, 400°F, for 5 minutes. Serve with the cooking juices, if made.

Serves 6-8 as a first course

Left: Sizzling Shrimp with Garlic and Chile
Right: Mussels with Prosciutto

STUFFED KIBBEH

Serve hot or cold with a green salad, yogurt and flat bread.

1⅓ CUPS FINE BURGHUL

½ LARGE ONION

1 LB LEAN TENDER LAMB, SUCH AS LEG,

DICED AND CHILLED

APPROXIMATELY ½ TEASPOON GROUND ALLSPICE

APPROXIMATELY ½ TEASPOON PEPPER

APPROXIMATELY 4 TABLESPOONS ICED WATER

OLIVE OIL FOR DEEP-FRYING

SALT

Filling

2 TABLESPOONS OIL

1 ONION, FINELY CHOPPED

3 TABLESPOONS PINE NUTS

½ LB LEAN LAMB, MINCED

½ TEASPOON ALLSPICE

1 TEASPOON GROUND CINNAMON

1 TABLESPOON EACH CHOPPED PARSLEY AND MINT

SALT AND PEPPER

Soak the burghul in cold water for 20 minutes. Drain and squeeze out the excess moisture. Using a food processor, finely chop the onion. Add the diced lamb and allspice, season and mix together. Add the burghul, mix again to a smooth, soft texture. To check the level of spicing, fry a very small piece and taste it. Knead the mixture well by hand.

To make the filling, heat the oil, add the onion and cook, stirring occasionally, until soft and becoming golden. Add the pine nuts and fry until golden. Stir in the minced lamb and cook, stirring occasionally, until the lamb has changed color and the juices evaporated. Add the remaining ingredients.

With oiled or wetted hands, take a piece of the kibbeh mixture about the size of an egg and form it into an egg shape. Holding it in the palm of one hand, make a small hole in it with the forefinger of the other hand and mould the kibbeh around and up the finger to make an oval shape with fairly thin walls. If the kibbeh cracks, repair it with a wetted finger – there must be no holes. Remove your finger.

Fill shell with about 1 tablespoon of the filling, then wet the rim of the opening and stick the edges together. Mould to a pointed oval. Repeat with remaining kibbeh and filling.

Deep-fry a few at a time in preheated oil, 350-375°F, for about 4 minutes until an even rich dark brown. Drain on paper towels.

Serves 4

CHICKEN STRIPS WITH FRESH MINT

In the eastern and southern Mediterranean countries, both fresh and dried spearmint (the variety of mint most often used) is popular. Usually it is home-dried in the hot sun and dry atmosphere; the dried leaves are rubbed between the hands so their warmth releases the herb's flavoring oils.

2 TABLESPOONS LEMON JUICE

1½ TEASPOONS OLIVE OIL

2 TABLESPOONS CHOPPED FRESH MINT OR

1 TABLESPOON DRIED MINT

2 CLOVES OF GARLIC, FINELY CHOPPED

1 LB SKINLESS CHICKEN BREAST, CUT ACROSS THE GRAIN

INTO ½ INCH THICK SLICES

SALT AND PEPPER

LETTUCE LEAVES TO SERVE

TOMATO WEDGES TO GARNISH

In a large shallow dish, combine the lemon juice, olive oil, mint, garlic and seasonings. Add the chicken, turn to coat with the lemon mixture, cover and leave for up to 2 hours at room temperature or up to 8 hours in the refrigerator. Return to room temperature 30 minutes before cooking.

If using wooden skewers, soak 4 or 5 that are 6 inches long in water for 30 minutes. Thread the pieces of chicken onto skewers, then cook under a preheated broiler or on a barbecue for 2½-3½ minutes each side. Serve on a bed of lettuce, garnished with tomato wedges.

Serves 4

ROAST VEGETABLE SALAD

All around the Mediterranean there is a tradition of cooking in the open air. Roasting a wide range of vegetables – onions, garlic, peppers, eggplants, zucchini, fennel, artichokes and so on – over the embers of a charcoal fire to give them a subdued complexity, deep, seductive smoky taste and silky texture is a high point of this way of cooking. Elsewhere most of us have to resort to baking the vegetables in the oven, and although the flavor will not be quite so beguiling, it is nevertheless very good.

2 SPANISH ONIONS, UNPEELED

1 LB SMALL EGGPLANTS

2 SWEET RED PEPPERS

3 FIRM BUT RIPE LARGE TOMATOES

8 CLOVES OF GARLIC

1 TEASPOON CUMIN SEEDS

3 TABLESPOONS LEMON JUICE

4 TABLESPOONS VIRGIN OLIVE OIL

3 TABLESPOONS WHITE WINE VINEGAR

2 TABLESPOONS FINELY CHOPPED PARSLEY OR TORN BASIL

SALT

Place the onions on a baking sheet and bake in a preheated oven, 350°F, for 10 minutes. Add the eggplants and bake for a further 10 minutes. Add the peppers and bake for 10 minutes before adding the tomatoes and 6 of the garlic cloves. Cook for a further 15 minutes, until all the vegetables are tender. If necessary, remove any vegetables that have cooked more quickly than the others. When the vegetables are cool enough to handle, peel them carefully with your fingers.

Cut the cores and seeds from the peppers and cut the flesh into strips. Halve the tomatoes, discard the seeds and slice the flesh. Slice the eggplants into strips and the onions into rings. Arrange the peppers, tomatoes, eggplants and onions in a serving dish.

Using a pestle and mortar or the end of a rolling pin in a small bowl, pound the roasted and raw garlic and the cumin seeds to a paste. Gradually beat in the lemon juice, oil and vinegar, then add salt to taste. Pour over the vegetables and sprinkle with parsley or basil. Serve warm or cold.

Serves 4

LAMBS' KIDNEYS IN SHERRY

Given the extent to which the recipe is known abroad, kidneys cooked with sherry is not served in tapas bars so often as might be expected. This is because the Spanish know that, to be worth eating, the dish must be freshly and quickly cooked with a deft hand – then it is truly delicious. These quantities serve 4 for tapas, but only 2-3 if you turn them into a meal and serve the dish with some good bread.

1 LB LAMBS' KIDNEYS

3 TABLESPOONS OLIVE OIL

2 CLOVES OF GARLIC, CHOPPED

1 CUP MUSHROOMS, CHOPPED

¼ CUP SERRANO HAM, CHOPPED

6-8 TABLESPOONS FINO SHERRY

SALT AND PEPPER

CHOPPED PARSLEY TO GARNISH

Remove the fine skin from the outside of each kidney, cut them in half lengthways and snip out and discard the cores. Quarter each kidney, then set aside.

Heat the oil in a frying pan, add the garlic and cook for 2-3 minutes, stirring occasionally. Stir in the mushrooms and fry until the liquid from the mushrooms has evaporated.

Stir the kidneys and ham into the pan and fry for 2-3 minutes, stirring frequently, so the kidneys are lightly browned on the outside but still pink in the center. Add the sherry and seasonings and boil, stirring occasionally, until the sherry has almost evaporated. Serve hot garnished with chopped parsley.

Serves 4

Eggs & Cheese

Eggs are used extensively in Mediterranean cooking in various forms – deep-fried, roasted, hard-boiled or added to casseroles. Alternatively, they may be scrambled with other ingredients or cooked with vegetables, ham, spicy sausage or cheese as a type of omelet such as a tortilla or frittata. The shortage of cattle in much of the region means that cheeses are more often made from ewes', goats' or water buffaloes' milk, and are, therefore, comparatively less plentiful.

EGGPLANT AND CHEESE SANDWICHES

The smell of a batch of these cooking drew me to a stall in Istanbul's fish market, where a boy, about 16 years old, was forming the "sandwiches," tossing them into the blackened pan of hot oil and always retrieving the right ones at the right moment, with all the aplomb of a seasoned expert. Anari is a Turkish whey cheese similar to ricotta; Mizithra a farmhouse-made, soft goats' or ewes' milk cheese.

1 EGGPLANT WEIGHING ¾ LB, CUT INTO ¼ INCH

ROUND SLICES

¼ LB ANARI OR MIZITHRA CHEESE, RICOTTA OR CREAM CHEESE

2 TABLESPOONS KEFALOTIRI OR PARMESAN CHEESE, FRESHLY GRATED

½ CLOVE OF GARLIC, CRUSHED

2 EGGS, BEATEN (SEPARATELY)

1½ TABLESPOONS CHOPPED MIXED HERBS SUCH AS PARSLEY,

MINT, DILL AND CHIVES

OLIVE OIL FOR COOKING

½ CUP TOASTED BREAD CRUMBS

SALT AND PEPPER

Sprinkle the eggplant slices with salt and leave in a colander for 30-60 minutes to drain. Rinse the slices and dry well.

Mash the cheeses and garlic with one of the beaten eggs, then mix in the herbs and seasonings.

Brush the eggplant slices with oil and cook under a preheated broiler until browned. Drain on paper towels.

Cut each eggplant slice in half. Spread the cheese mixture on half of these then cover neatly with the remaining halves and press lightly together.

Put the toasted bread crumbs into a shallow dish and the remaining beaten egg into a bowl. Dip the eggplant "sandwiches" in the egg, allow excess to drain off and coat evenly with bread crumbs.

Fry in hot olive oil for about 1½ minutes each side, until golden and crisp. Drain the "sandwiches" on paper towels and serve hot garnished with finely chopped herbs such as dill, or parsley and mint.

Serves 3-4

FRIED MANCHEGO CHEESE FRITTERS

When these fritters are made with good Manchego cheese, properly fried and freshly cooked so that they are crisp and deliciously savory, I find them extremely difficult to resist.

Manchego is sometimes referred to as the Spanish equivalent of Cheddar, but it is more like Parmesan, as it, too, is made from ewes' milk, and rivals the Italian cheese for superiority when well made and matured.

OLIVE OIL FOR DEEP-FRYING

2 EGG WHITES

1 CUP MATURE MANCHEGO CHEESE, FINELY GRATED

1 CUP FRESH BREAD CRUMBS

ABOUT 1 TABLESPOON FINELY CHOPPED FRESH HERBS SUCH AS PARSLEY,

CHIVES AND THYME

PAPRIKA

SALT AND PEPPER

Heat a deep-fryer two thirds full with olive oil to 350-375°F.

Meanwhile, in a clean bowl, whisk the egg whites until stiff but not dry. Using a large metal spoon, lightly fold in the grated cheese, bread crumbs and herbs. Season with salt, pepper and paprika.

Form the cheese mixture into small walnut-sized balls, adding the balls to the hot oil in the deep-fryer as they are shaped, but do not overcrowd the pan. Fry for about 3 minutes, until golden.

When cooked transfer the fritters to paper towels to drain. Serve hot.

Serves 4

Overleaf:
From left to right: Eggplant and Cheese Sandwiches, Fried Manchego Cheese Fritters and Basil and Cheese Frittata

BASIL AND CHEESE FRITTATA

With just fragrant basil and good Parmesan cheese, this most simple of frittata recipes is possibly my favorite.

7 EGGS

3 TABLESPOONS FRESHLY GRATED PARMESAN CHEESE

4 TABLESPOONS TORN BASIL LEAVES

3 TABLESPOONS UNSALTED BUTTER

SALT AND PEPPER

Using a fork, lightly beat the eggs with the cheese, basil, salt and pepper until the yolks and whites are blended.

Heat the butter in a 12 inch heavy frying pan over a moderate heat until it begins to foam. Pour in the eggs and reduce the heat to very low. Cook very gently for about 15 minutes until the bulk is almost set, with only the top of the frittata still creamy and moist. Place under a preheated broiler for 30-60 seconds until just set.

Loosen the edges of the frittata with a spatula and slide it onto a warm plate. Serve cut into wedges.

Serves 4

Variations

Asparagus Frittata – use 6 eggs and ½ cup Parmesan cheese. Omit the basil, but add 3 cups cooked asparagus cut into ½ inch lengths.

Zucchini Eggah – salt 5 coarsely grated zucchini, drain in a colander for 30-60 minutes, then rinse and dry. Cook a chopped onion gently in olive oil in a 10 inch frying pan until very soft and golden. Add 1 crushed garlic clove, cook until aromatic, then stir in the zucchini and cook over a moderate heat, stirring until tender. Pour in 5 lightly beaten eggs, approximately 3 tablespoons chopped dill, and pepper, then cook as above.

Spinach Eggah – cook and drain 1 lb fresh spinach or 1 cup thawed frozen spinach. Lightly mix with 6 eggs, freshly grated nutmeg and salt and pepper. Cook as above in 4 tablespoons butter in a 12 inch frying pan.

HAMINE EGGS WITH FUL MEDAMES

Hamine Eggs have a unique flavor and creamy consistency that results from long, slow cooking. Onion skins added to the cooking water color the eggs fawn. They are traditionally served with Ful Medames, made from a type of small dried fava bean which is a speciality of Egypt.

HAMINE EGGS

4 EGGS

SKINS OF 3-4 LARGE ONIONS

FUL MEDAMES

1 CUP DRIED FUL BEANS, SOAKED OVERNIGHT

JUST COVERED BY COLD WATER

3 TABLESPOONS OLIVE OIL

3 CLOVES OF GARLIC, FINELY CHOPPED

1½ TABLESPOONS CHOPPED PARSLEY OR CILANTRO

2-3 TABLESPOONS LEMON JUICE

4 SCALLIONS, WHITE PART ONLY, CHOPPED

SALT AND PEPPER

TO SERVE

CHOPPED PARSLEY

LEMON JUICE

OLIVE OIL

For the hamine eggs, put the eggs and onion skins in a large saucepan. Cover generously with water, bring slowly to the boil, cover and simmer gently for 5-6 hours, or overnight. Keep an eye on the water level to ensure eggs are always covered – a layer of oil poured over the surface of the water will slow down the evaporation. A slow cooker is useful.

Drain the eggs and shell when cool enough to handle.

Meanwhile, drain the beans, put them into a heavy casserole dish or saucepan, just cover with water, cover the casserole dish or pan tightly and simmer very gently for 5-6 hours, or until tender. If the beans become too dry during cooking, pour in a little water but do not stir; at the end of cooking there should be hardly any spare liquid.

Tip the beans into a bowl, stir in the oil, garlic, parsley or cilantro, lemon juice, salt and pepper. Let cool then stir in the scallions. Serve in soup bowls with the eggs on top, and sprinkled with parsley. Traditionally each person crushes their bowlful of beans and eggs with a fork, mixing them together and adding extra lemon juice, olive oil and seasoning to taste.

Serves 4

MARINATED BALLS OF LABNE

*Labne, laban, labna or labneh is Middle Eastern strained
yogurt, traditionally made from ewes' or water buffaloes'
milk. It is popular for breakfast spread on to opened out
pita bread, or as a mezze, when it is seasoned with salt and
pepper or paprika and sprinkled with dill or mint, before
being spread on pita bread, trickled with oil and eaten with
olives. It is also rolled into balls, packed into jars and
covered with olive oil. I often flavor the balls with paprika
or finely chopped mint, cilantro, parsley, dill, or a mixture.
Alternatively, sprigs of herbs, and/or
a couple of split cloves of garlic can be added to the
jar with the oil.*

1-1½ TEASPOONS SALT

4 CUPS YOGURT MADE FROM EWES' MILK

OR WHOLE COWS' MILK

OLIVE OIL (OPTIONAL)

To make labne, stir the salt into the yogurt. Spoon it into
the centre of a double thickness of cheesecloth or piece of
fine cotton, gather up the corners of the cloth, tie them
securely and suspend over a bowl. Leave in a cool place to
drain for at least 10 hours.

When the yogurt has reached the consistency of ricotta
cheese, scoop up spoonfuls and roll them into smooth balls.
Leave in the refrigerator for several hours until firm and a
little dried. (If you are not making balls of labne, simply
transfer it to a bowl or pots, cover and refrigerate.)

Pack the labne balls into a clean jar and cover with olive
oil. Close the jar tightly and store at room temperature. If
serving as a mezze, serve the balls in a bowl with a little of
the oil, so that it can be used to soften the cheese.

The labne balls can be kept for up to 3 weeks.

Serves 4

Variation

Marinated Goats' Cheese – put 6 small, firm, but not dry
goats' cheeses in a wide-necked jar with 1 tablespoon
peppercorns, 2 small dried red chiles, 4 bay leaves and
3 sprigs of thyme. Cover with olive oil, close the jar and
leave for 1-2 weeks; the longer the cheeses are left the
stronger the flavor will become and the harder they will get.
Eat within 3 months.

CHAKCHOUKA

*The inclusion of hot red chiles pinpoints this, the most spicy
of the egg dishes, as Tunisian.*

3 TABLESPOONS OLIVE OIL

1 SPANISH ONION, THINLY SLICED

3 CUPS SWEET RED PEPPERS, CORED, DESEEDED AND SLICED

1-2 FRESH RED CHILES, DESEEDED AND CHOPPED

5 RIPE TOMATOES, SKINNED, DESEEDED AND CHOPPED

PINCH OF SUGAR (OPTIONAL)

4 EGGS

SALT AND PEPPER

Heat the oil in a deep heavy frying or sauté pan, add the
onion and cook gently until it softens and begins to color.
Add the peppers and chiles and cook, stirring occasionally,
until almost soft. Stir in the tomatoes and cook for a further
8 minutes or so until all the vegetables are soft but the
mixture has not become a mush. Add salt and pepper and a
little sugar, if necessary.

Make 4 deep depressions in the vegetable mixture, break
in the eggs, cover the pan and cook gently until the eggs are
set to the required degree, basting once or twice with the
juices. Serve immediately.

Serves 4

Variation

Huevos a la Flamenca – cook ½ a finely chopped Spanish
onion and 2 cloves of crushed garlic until soft. Add 2 slices
of chopped serrano ham and 1 chopped sweet red pepper,
cook for 2 minutes, then add 1 teaspoon paprika. After
30 seconds, stir in 2 skinned, deseeded and chopped
tomatoes. Simmer to a thickish purée. Add ½ cup cooked
fresh or frozen peas, ½ cup cooked green beans and a little
tomato paste, if necessary. Season to taste. Pour into a
shallow ovenproof dish or 4 individual dishes. Form
4 shallow depressions and break an egg into each. Scatter
over 2 slices chopped serrano ham and lay a chorizo slice on
the yolks. Cook in a preheated oven, 450°F, for 8-10
minutes for egg whites that are just set but with still moist
yolks. Cook for 15 minutes for firmer eggs. Sprinkle over a
little parsley before serving.

*From left to right:
Hamine Eggs with Ful Medames,
Marinated Balls of Labne and Chakchouka*

46

PIPERADE

The regional pepper to use for Piperade is the "piment d'Espelletes," grown around the town of the same name in the Pays Basque, and the center for the cultivation of several varieties of sweetish or hottish red peppers and in the business of sun-drying and selling them. The ham can be fried if preferred and the eggs mixed with all the vegetables. Serve for a light main course, a snack or supper dish, especially in summer.

4 THIN SLICES OF BAYONNE HAM

2 TABLESPOONS OLIVE OIL

1 SPANISH ONION, CHOPPED

2 CLOVES OF GARLIC, CHOPPED

1 SWEET GREEN PEPPER, CHARRED, CORED, DESEEDED AND SLICED

1 SWEET RED PEPPER, CHARRED, CORED, DESEEDED AND SLICED

5 VERY RIPE TOMATOES, SKINNED, DESEEDED AND CHOPPED

6-8 EGGS

SALT AND PEPPER

Trim the fat from the ham. Reserve the ham, dice the fat and heat with the oil in a heavy-bottomed frying pan. Add the onion and garlic and cook, stirring occasionally, until softened but not colored. Stir in the peppers and tomatoes, season and simmer gently for about 15 minutes, stirring occasionally, until lightly thickened. Transfer two thirds of the vegetables to a saucepan, cover and keep warm. Place the slices of ham under a low broiler to warm.

Stir the eggs into the frying pan and cook over a low heat, stirring gently, until the eggs begin to thicken. Remove immediately from the heat. Place a slice of ham in each of 4 warm deep plates, place a quarter of the vegetable mixture on top, add the egg mixture and serve immediately.

Serves 4

MENEMEN

Menemen takes its name from a small coastal town in western Turkey. "Sivri biber" are the best peppers to use – long and pale with thin, moderately hot tasting flesh. I have seen them in shops selling Turkish foods in this country, but if you are unable to buy them, use milder green chiles or a mixture of ordinary sweet green peppers and hot green chiles. Sometimes "beyaz peynir," the local feta cheese, which is softer than those we usually get here, is sprinkled over the mixture when it is almost ready to give a more savory and sustaining dish; then a scattering of parsley finishes the dish.

2 TABLESPOONS OIL

¼ LB SWEET GREEN PEPPER, OR A COMBINATION OF SWEET AND CHILE PEPPERS, CORED, DESEEDED AND FINELY CHOPPED

2 LARGE, VERY RIPE YET FIRM TOMATOES, SKINNED, DESEEDED AND CHOPPED

4 EGGS, BEATEN

SALT

WARM PITA BREAD TO SERVE

Heat the oil in a small frying pan, add the pepper and chile, if using, and the tomatoes and cook over a moderate heat for 5-6 minutes until the pepper has relaxed and the tomato has begun to dry out. Sprinkle with salt.

Lower the heat, stir in the beaten eggs and continue to stir gently until the eggs are beginning to set but are still creamy. Serve the Menemen immediately with warm pita bread to mop up the juices.

Serves 2

EGGS IN SPINACH

Served with a tomato or sweet red pepper salad and crusty bread, this Turkish recipe makes a tasty lunch or supper dish. A lighter, less savory version can be made by omitting the cheese and, instead, sprinkling a little olive oil over each uncooked egg, then serving with thick yogurt. To serve as a first course, you could use individual flameproof earthenware dishes, such as cazuelas, or divide the spinach mixture between 4 ovenproof dishes, break the eggs into these and bake in a preheated oven, 350°F, for about 15 minutes until the eggs are set to the firmness you like.

1 LB FRESH SPINACH, STALKS REMOVED

2 TABLESPOONS OLIVE OIL

1 ONION, FINELY CHOPPED

1 CLOVE OF GARLIC, FINELY CHOPPED

4 EGGS

¼ LB FETA CHEESE

SALT AND PEPPER

CHOPPED WHITE AND GREEN PARTS OF SCALLIONS

OR PAPRIKA TO SERVE

Wash and drain, but do not dry the spinach. Shred it and place in a large saucepan. Heat, stirring occasionally, until it is wilted and there is no spare liquid visible. Tip into a colander and press to extract as much liquid as possible.

Heat the oil in a heavy frying pan and cook the onion until transparent and lightly browned, add the garlic. Stir in the spinach towards the end of cooking and keep stirring for a few minutes. Season with pepper and a very little salt, depending on the saltiness of the cheese.

With the back of a spoon make 4 hollows in the spinach mixture. Break an egg into each depression. Crumble the cheese over the entire surface and grind over black pepper. Heat over a medium heat until steaming, then cover with a lid and leave for 5-10 minutes until the eggs are set to the required degree. Sprinkle with chopped scallions or paprika. Serve hot or warm.
Serves 2

FRIED CHEESE AND EGGS

In Greece the recipe is named after the dish in which it is cooked and served – saganaki. In the ouzeries, one large slice of cheese is fried in a saganaki and served individually at table. There, hard dry Kashkaval or Kasseri cheese is used; in Sicily, I have been served fried Pecorino Sardo cheese and eggs and no doubt, other cheeses are given the same treatment. The oil may be flavored by frying garlic and/or dried red chile in it first, if you like.

4 FINGER-THICK SLICES OF HARD CHEESE SUCH AS KASSERI OR PECORINO

2 TABLESPOONS OLIVE OIL

4 EGGS

SALT AND PEPPER

Fry the cheese in hot oil in a heavy frying pan just large enough to hold the 4 slices. When the cheese begins to melt and bubble, break an egg over each slice and continue to cook until the white has set. Serve immediately, sprinkled with salt and pepper.
Serves 4

Variation
Cut thick slices from a block of halumi cheese and pat dry with paper towels. Marinate in olive oil with thyme or cilantro and pepper for at least 30 minutes, before frying in the marinating oil.

To give the cheese a crisp coating, and also prevent cheese that is not sufficiently hard from melting too quickly, press polenta into the slices before frying. Fry the eggs in a separate pan then serve on top of the cheese. With this variation, mozzarella cheese can be used.

Vegetables & Salads

Vegetables are the glory of the Mediterranean diet – bought with care and close scrutiny, cherished, treated with respect and eaten with relish. The rich repertoire of varied and well-flavored dishes, enhanced by the skilful use of herbs, spices and other flavorings, includes vegetables that are broiled, boiled, deep-fried, stuffed, baked, added to omelets, tarts and pies, transformed into richly flavored, colorful casseroles, or tossed with dressings and served as warm or cold salads.

WARM SALADE NICOISE

It is impossible to give a definitive recipe for Salade Niçoise as there is a lot of controversy over what can and cannot be included in an authentic one. This one will be greeted with horror by any traditionalists, but I've included it not just to be contentious, but because it makes a very good dish, and one that is far better than many a so-called Salade Niçoise.

5 SMALL NEW POTATOES, SCRUBBED,

OR 2 MEDIUM POTATOES, SCRUBBED AND QUARTERED

5 TABLESPOONS VIRGIN OLIVE OIL

2 TABLESPOONS RED WINE VINEGAR

½ LB GREEN BEANS, TOPPED AND TAILED

½ LB FRESH TUNA STEAK, CUT INTO FINGER STRIPS

2 CLOVES OF GARLIC, FINELY CHOPPED

2 ANCHOVY FILLETS, CHOPPED

APPROXIMATELY 1½ TEASPOONS DIJON MUSTARD

1 SWEET RED PEPPER, CHARRED, SKINNED, DESEEDED AND THINLY SLICED

2 TABLESPOONS CAPERS

SALT AND PEPPER

LEMON WEDGES TO SERVE (OPTIONAL)

Steam the potatoes for 8-10 minutes, until just tender. Transfer to a serving bowl and toss gently with 1 tablespoon each of the oil and the vinegar, and salt and pepper.

Steam the green beans for 5-6 minutes until just tender. Set aside.

Heat 1 tablespoon of the oil in a non-stick frying pan, add the tuna and sear evenly over a high heat. Add to the potato mixture. Add the remaining oil to the frying pan, then stir in the garlic and anchovies for 30 seconds. Stir in the remaining vinegar and boil for 1 minute or so. Stir in the mustard, then pour over the potato mixture. Add the pepper strips, beans, capers and more black pepper. Toss gently, taste and adjust the flavorings if necessary, then serve immediately with lemon wedges, if you like.

Serves 2 as a main course

MUSHROOM AND CHEESE SALAD

In some versions of the recipe, the mushrooms are marinated in oil and vinegar or lemon juice; in others, olive oil alone is used, while other recipes merely sprinkle sliced mushrooms with oil. If you use lemon juice or vinegar, be sure to balance it against the oil so that there is just enough acidity to give the salad the sharpness it needs to contrast with the mushrooms. It is also important not to swamp the salad with dressing. The texture and flavor of porcini (ceps) really do make quite a difference, but, of course, money and season do not always permit such perfection so, on these occasions, I recommend substituting oyster or cremini mushrooms. Serve as an antipasto, a simple lunch or with poultry or white meat.

2½ CUPS PORCINI (CEPS), OYSTER OR LARGE CREMINI

MUSHROOMS, THINLY SLICED

½ CUP PARMESAN CHEESE, SHAVED

10 BASIL LEAVES, TORN

DRESSING

3 TABLESPOONS OLIVE OIL

1 TABLESPOON LEMON JUICE OR WHITE WINE VINEGAR

SALT AND PEPPER

Arrange the mushrooms on a large serving plate. Scatter over the cheese, then the basil.

Make the dressing; whisk together the oil, lemon juice or vinegar and salt and pepper and pour evenly over the salad. Serve at once or leave for 30 minutes.

Serves 4

Variation

Fava Bean and Pecorino Salad – blanch 3 lb fresh shelled fava beans in boiling salted water for 1 minute. Drain, then mix with 2 cups diced Pecorino Romano, 3 tablespoons olive oil and black pepper.

Overleaf:
Left: Warm Salad Niçoise
Right: Mushroom and Cheese Salad

MOZZARELLA AND TOMATO SALAD

As the concept is simple and the basic ingredients readily available, this has become a very popular salad, especially with restaurants. However, whether it tastes any good rests entirely on the quality of the raw materials. On the island of its birth, Capri, where the salad is known as Caprese, really fresh buffalo mozzarella, sun-soaked, juicy tomatoes, rich olive oil and well-flavored basil are used, and it can be a truly memorable salad – quite unlike the versions served elsewhere with rubbery cheese, tasteless, watery tomatoes and oil and basil that lack character. This is a salad to be eaten immediately or, at least, within 30 minutes. Although not quite the genuine Caprese, really good, pitted black olives and fat capers may also be scattered over.

¼ LB VERY FRESH BUFFALO MOZZARELLA CHEESE, THICKLY SLICED

2-3 EXTRA LARGE TOMATOES, THICKLY SLICED

LEAVES FROM A LARGE BUNCH BASIL, TORN

EXTRA-VIRGIN OLIVE OIL

SALT AND PEPPER

Arrange alternate slices of mozzarella cheese and tomato in circles on 4 small plates or 1 large one. Scatter over the torn basil leaves.

Season the olive oil with salt and black pepper and trickle over the salads.

Serves 4

GREEK COUNTRY SALAD

Greek tavernas worldwide serve what could be dubbed as Greece's national salad, Horiatiki Salata. Purists say that it should be made with two types of lettuce – romaine and boston, the former shredded, the latter torn. They should be tossed with oil in a large bowl, then the other ingredients carefully added in layers of contrasting colors. Finally, the dressing is trickled over the top. The bowl is then placed in the center of the table and each person dips in their fork, taking what they fancy.

4 TABLESPOONS OLIVE OIL

1 TABLESPOON RED WINE VINEGAR

1 CLOVE OF GARLIC, CRUSHED

½ CUCUMBER, PEELED IF LIKED

1 SMALL BOSTON LETTUCE, TORN

1 SMALL ROMAINE LETTUCE, SHREDDED

3 FIRM BUT RIPE TOMATOES, CUT INTO WEDGES

1 SPANISH ONION, THINLY SLICED INTO RINGS

1 SWEET GREEN PEPPER, CORED, DESEEDED AND THINLY SLICED INTO RINGS

½ CUP FETA CHEESE, CRUMBLED

12 OR MORE BLACK KALAMATA OLIVES

12 TABLESPOONS COARSELY CHOPPED PARSLEY

2 TEASPOONS CHOPPED OREGANO

SALT AND PEPPER

Vigorously whisk together the oil, vinegar, garlic and salt and pepper. Leave for 1 hour.

Halve the cucumber lengthways, scoop out the seeds and thinly slice the cucumber. Sprinkle with salt and leave to drain. Rinse the cucumber and dry with paper towels.

Whisk the oil and vinegar again, then toss a little of it with the lettuces in a bowl. Layer the tomatoes, cucumber, onion, pepper, cheese and olives on the lettuce. Pour over the remaining dressing then scatter over the chopped parsley and the oregano.

Serves 4

EGGPLANT CANNELLONI

The "cannelloni" are formed from slices of eggplant cut along the length of the vegetable. They are filled with a simple, light mixture of soft goats' and ricotta cheeses flavored with basil, then topped with a tomato sauce, to make a dish that is tasty and satisfying without being too heavy.

4 EGGPLANTS, ABOUT ½ LB EACH

OLIVE OIL FOR BRUSHING

1 CUP RICOTTA CHEESE

1 CUP SOFT GOATS' CHEESE

1 CUP PARMESAN CHEESE, FRESHLY GRATED

4 TABLESPOONS CHOPPED BASIL

SAUCE

2 TABLESPOONS OLIVE OIL

1 ONION, CHOPPED

2 CLOVES OF GARLIC, CRUSHED

6 SUN-RIPENED TOMATOES, SKINNED, DESEEDED AND CHOPPED

½ CUP VEGETABLE OR CHICKEN STOCK,

MEDIUM-BODIED DRY WHITE WINE, OR WATER

APPROXIMATELY 1 TABLESPOON SUN-DRIED TOMATO PASTE

SALT AND PEPPER

TO GARNISH

SHAVED PARMESAN CHEESE

BASIL SPRIGS

To make the sauce, heat the oil in a saucepan, add the onion and cook gently, stirring occasionally, until soft. Stir in the garlic, tomatoes, stock, wine or water, and tomato paste then simmer until thickened to a fairly light sauce. Season.

Meanwhile, thinly slice the eggplants lengthways and brush lightly with oil. Cook under a preheated broiler until evenly browned on both sides. Drain on paper towels.

Mix together the cheeses, chopped basil and seasoning to taste. Spoon the cheese mixture along the eggplants and roll the slices, from the short end, around the filling. Place the rolls, seam-side down, in a single layer in a shallow baking dish and place in a preheated oven, 375°F, for about 10-15 minutes, until the filling is hot. Reheat the sauce if necessary.

Divide the "cannelloni" between warmed plates, spoon the sauce across the eggplant rolls, scatter over the shaved Parmesan cheese and garnish with basil sprigs.

Serves 6-8 as a first course, 4 as a main course

ARTICHOKE AND FAVA BEAN STEW

One of my strongest memories of Crete is driving late one evening, when the sun was a fast-sinking glowing ball, through endless eerie fields "policed" by tall, stately, globe artichoke plants topped by their spiked caps. Next day, we lunched at a taverna just outside Fourfouras, which served artichokes in innumerable ways. We sat under the vines, nibbled home-pickled artichoke hearts and sipped ouzo while making our choice. I chose this dish of delicious home-grown artichokes and beans with rich cooking juices which came with thick slices of country bread.

4 ARTICHOKES

½ LEMON

4 TABLESPOONS VIRGIN OLIVE OIL, PLUS EXTRA FOR SPRINKLING

1 SMALL ONION, FINELY CHOPPED

3 CUPS SHELLED FRESH SMALL FAVA BEANS (OR THAWED FROZEN BEANS)

APPROXIMATELY 1½ TABLESPOONS CHOPPED MINT OR DILL

2 TABLESPOONS WATER

SALT AND PEPPER

TO SERVE (OPTIONAL)

CHOPPED PARSLEY

FRESHLY GRATED KEFALOTIRI CHEESE

Snap the stems from the artichokes and pull away the outer leaves to leave a cone of soft small leaves in the center. Cut off the soft cone and cut away the hairy choke. Cut each bottom lengthways into quarters, then cut each quarter in half lengthways. Rub all the cut surfaces with the half lemon.

In a saucepan just large enough to hold the vegetables, heat the oil. Add the onion, cook for 2-3 minutes and then add the artichokes. Stir around for 4-5 minutes before covering and cooking over a moderate heat, shaking the pan occasionally, until the artichokes are almost half cooked, about 5 minutes. Add the fresh beans, mint or dill, water and seasoning, cover tightly and cook for about 10 minutes, depending on the age and size of the beans, shaking the pan occasionally, until the vegetables are tender. (If using frozen beans, add them when the artichokes are almost tender and cook for a further 4-5 minutes.)

Serve in warm, deep plates. Grind black pepper over the top, sprinkle with chopped parsley, a few drops of olive oil and a little cheese if you like.

Serves 4

Left: Eggplant Canneloni
Right: Artichoke and Fava Bean Stew

RATATOUILLE

*The name ratatouille is derived from two slang words –
"rata" in French army parlance means simple rations, and
"touiller" meaning to stir or mix. The flavor develops with
time and it is delicious with meats or poultry, broiled
polenta, poached eggs, tossed with pasta, as a filling for
omelets, or if thick, for small savory pastries.*

2 EGGPLANTS

3 ZUCCHINI, SLICED

7 TABLESPOONS OLIVE OIL

1 SPANISH ONION, VERY THINLY SLICED

3 CLOVES OF GARLIC, CRUSHED

2 LARGE SWEET RED PEPPERS, CORED, DESEEDED AND THINLY SLICED

4 LARGE SUN-RIPENED TOMATOES, SKINNED, DESEEDED AND CHOPPED

LEAVES FROM A FEW SPRIGS OF THYME, MARJORAM AND OREGANO

ABOUT 2 TABLESPOONS EACH OF CHOPPED PARSLEY AND TORN BASIL LEAVES

SALT AND PEPPER

Halve each eggplant lengthways and cut into slices about
1 inch thick. Sprinkle salt over the eggplant and zucchini
slices, place in a colander and leave for 1 hour. Rinse well
then dry thoroughly with paper towels.

Heat 2 tablespoons of the oil in a heavy flameproof
casserole dish, add the eggplant and sauté for a few minutes.
Add another tablespoon of the oil and the onion and garlic
and sauté for a few minutes. Add the red peppers and cook,
stirring occasionally, for a minute or so. Add another
2 tablespoons of the oil and the zucchini. Cook, stirring
occasionally, for a few minutes. Add the tomatoes, snip in
the herb leaves, season lightly and add the remaining
2 tablespoons of oil. Cover the casserole dish and cook very
gently for 30-40 minutes, stirring occasionally. Stir in the
parsley and basil and cook, uncovered, for 5-10 minutes until
there is no surplus liquid. Serve warm or cold.

Serves 4

Variation
Peperonata – soften 1 chopped onion and 2 chopped
cloves of garlic in 4 tablespoons of oil in a large frying pan.
Stir in 2-3 skinned, deseeded and chopped extra large
tomatoes and cook gently for 10-15 minutes until thickened.
Stir in 4 charred, cored and sliced sweet red peppers and
cook for a further 5 minutes or so, until the peppers are
soft. Add salt and pepper to taste and sugar if necessary to
give a rich flavor. Cool for about 5 minutes before serving
sprinkled with parsley.

BRAISED BROCCOLI WITH GARLIC

*This old-fashioned, southern Italian way of cooking broccoli
slowly and gently produces a very different vegetable from
the one that is currently in vogue. Instead of being crisp,
the broccoli melts on the tongue, as does the garlic. Chiles
and sun-dried tomatoes or olives add a contrasting
piquancy that lifts the dish. Serve as a first course, an
accompaniment to a plain main course or for a light lunch
or supper dish.*

1 SMALL BUNCH (1½ LB) BROCCOLI

4 TABLESPOONS OLIVE OIL

6 CLOVES OF GARLIC

2 DRIED RED CHILES, DESEEDED AND COARSELY CHOPPED

4 HALVES OF SUN-DRIED TOMATOES, OR 8 BLACK OLIVES, HALVED AND PITTED

1 CUP WHITE WINE OR WATER

⅓ CUP PECORINO ROMANO OR PARMESAN CHEESE, SHAVED THINLY

Trim the woody ends from the broccoli and discard. Leave
slim pieces of broccoli whole, but slice thicker stems in half
or quarters along their length.

Pour the oil into a wide heavy saucepan, stir in the
broccoli, garlic, chiles and sun-dried tomatoes or olives. Add
the wine or water, cover and cook over a low heat for 45-
60 minutes until the liquid has almost completely
evaporated; if necessary, uncover the pan towards the end.

Tip into a warm dish and scatter over the cheese.

Serves 4

SPICED CASSEROLE OF SWEET POTATOES AND PEAS

I have subdued the original flavorings of this Tunisian recipe so that the combination of lemon juice, honey, cinnamon and chiles subtly complements the flavor of sweet potatoes, but if you prefer a dish with a punchier flavor, increase their quantities.

4 TABLESPOONS LEMON JUICE

3-4 TEASPOONS CLEAR HONEY

1 TEASPOON GROUND CINNAMON

¾ TEASPOON CHILE POWDER, OR TO TASTE

2 TABLESPOONS OLIVE OIL

1½ LB SWEET POTATOES, CUT INTO ½ INCH CUBES

1 ONION, FINELY CHOPPED

2 CLOVES OF GARLIC, FINELY CHOPPED

4 TABLESPOONS WATER

SALT

Mix together 1 tablespoon of the lemon juice, all of the honey, cinnamon and chile powder. Set aside.

Heat the oil in a large, heavy frying pan, add the sweet potatoes and cook, stirring occasionally, for 10 minutes. Add the onion, garlic, salt, remaining lemon juice and water. Cook, stirring occasionally, for about 5 minutes until the onion begins to brown. Add the spiced honey mixture, cook, stirring, for 2 minutes, then serve.

Serves 4

Variation

Tunisian Spiced Carrots – to serve hot or cold. Boil 2 lb sliced young carrots for about 3 minutes. Drain. Soften 1 chopped onion and 2 cloves of garlic in olive oil. Add the carrots, ½ cup vegetable or chicken stock, 1 teaspoon each clear honey, harissa, cumin and coriander and season to taste. Cook for a further 10-12 minutes. Stir in chopped parsley before serving.

BRAISED FENNEL WITH CHEESE

In Florence, Italy, fennel used to be eaten at the end of the meal, as it was believed to help digestion and was therefore a fitting food with which to round off a heavy or rich meal. This practice has virtually vanished, with the exception of a few places in Tuscany, where sliced fennel is served as a digestif, sometimes with mandarins or other oranges. Nowadays, fennel appears frequently in baked vegetable dishes, including this one, which, though simple, is one of the best.

4 BULBS OF YOUNG FENNEL

3 TABLESPOONS LEMON JUICE

¼ CUP UNSALTED BUTTER, CUBED

1 TABLESPOON VIRGIN OLIVE OIL

½ CUP PARMESAN CHEESE, FRESHLY GRATED,

OR GORGONZOLA CHEESE, CRUMBLED

SALT AND PEPPER

BROWNED FLAKED ALMONDS, OR CHOPPED TOASTED WALNUTS TO GARNISH

Trim and reserve the feathery fennel fronds. Cut the fennel into quarters and boil in salted water to which the lemon juice has been added for about 15 minutes, until tender but still crisp. Drain through a colander and place on paper towels to drain further.

Place the fennel in a single layer in a baking dish, scatter over the butter and olive oil, sprinkle with the cheese, season with plenty of black pepper then place, uncovered, in a preheated oven, 400°F, for about 20 minutes until brown. Serve with the nuts scattered over.

Serves 4

CATALAN SPINACH WITH RAISINS AND PINE NUTS

Pine nuts and raisins signal the Arab influence that lies behind this interesting Spanish treatment of spinach; the leaves of Swiss chard may also be cooked in this way. Serve as a vegetable accompaniment or as a first course accompanied by croutons.

3 TABLESPOONS OLIVE OIL

⅓ CUP TOASTED PINE NUTS

1½ LB FRESH SPINACH, STALKS REMOVED

1-2 CLOVES OF GARLIC, CHOPPED

¼ CUP RAISINS

SALT AND PEPPER

Heat 1 tablespoon of the oil in a small saucepan, add the pine nuts and fry until golden. Using a slotted spoon, transfer to paper towels to drain.

Heat the remaining oil in a large saucepan. Wash, but do not dry the spinach, add to the pan with the garlic and cook over a high heat for about 5 minutes, stirring with a wooden spoon, until wilted and there is no excess moisture visible. Stir in the pine nuts, raisins and seasonings and cook for a couple of minutes.

Serves 4

From top to bottom: Tumbet, Stuffed Onions and Catalan Spinach with Raisins and Pine Nuts

TUMBET

My first experience of Tumbet was in Valldemossa, Majorca, where as hard-up students we each ate just a single dish of it, to the consternation of the restaurant proprietor, who considered it an accompaniment to a main dish of broiled meat. For us, however, Tumbet had the virtues of being cheap and filling as well as very tasty.

3 EGGPLANTS

OLIVE OIL FOR COOKING

2 ONIONS, CHOPPED

3 CLOVES OF GARLIC, CRUSHED

4 LARGE SUN-RIPENED TOMATOES, SKINNED, DESEEDED AND CHOPPED

2-3 SPRIGS OF OREGANO OR MARJORAM

2 LARGE POTATOES, CUT INTO SLICES

SUGAR (OPTIONAL)

2 SWEET RED PEPPERS, CORED, DESEEDED AND SLICED

SALT AND PEPPER

CRUSTY BREAD TO SERVE

Quarter the eggplants lengthways, then halve each piece. Place in a colander, sprinkle evenly with salt and leave for 30-60 minutes to drain.

Heat about 2 tablespoons of oil, add the onions and garlic, fry gently until softened and lightly browned. Stir in the tomatoes, oregano or marjoram and simmer for about 15 minutes.

Meanwhile, heat a thin layer of oil in a large frying pan, add a single layer of potato slices and cook over a moderate heat until golden on both sides and about three-quarters cooked. Remove with a slotted spoon, drain on paper towels and put into a flameproof earthenware casserole dish. Repeat with the remaining potatoes.

Season the tomato sauce and add a little sugar if necessary. Pour about one third over the potatoes.

Rinse and dry the eggplant pieces and fry in batches in the frying pan until golden. Using a slotted spoon, transfer to paper towels to drain, then add to the casserole dish. Pour over another third of the tomato sauce.

Fry pepper slices in the pan and add to the casserole dish. Pour over the remaining sauce. Almost cover, leaving a small gap for steam to escape. Simmer very gently for 15-20 minutes until the potatoes are tender and the sauce thick.

Alternatively, bake, uncovered, in a preheated oven, 350°F, for 15 minutes. Let stand for 5-10 minutes before serving or cool to room temperature. Serve with plenty of crusty bread to mop up the juices.

Serves 4

STUFFED ONIONS

One year I stayed with friends who have an old farmhouse in the foothills of the Pyrenees. One chilly Sunday morning we went to the open-air market set beneath a canopy of sycamore trees in Ceret, a favorite haunt of Picasso. We behaved like tourists, buying Catalan cotton espadrilles and yards of brightly colored fabrics (which have still not been made into anything!), and eating cechi, the local cream-filled doughnuts fried to order, as we wandered. We also bought large loaves of whole wheat bread to eat with the stuffed onions we had left in the old, heavy oven. By the time we got home, the large onions had been rendered mellow, sweet, succulent and unforgettable by the long, slow cooking.

4 LARGE ONIONS, AROUND ¾ LB EACH EACH, UNPEELED

½ CUP SOFT GOATS' CHEESE

4 SUN-DRIED TOMATOES, SOAKED IF NECESSARY, CHOPPED

2 EGG YOLKS

½ TEASPOON CRUMBLED THYME

2 TABLESPOONS CHOPPED PARSLEY

2 TABLESPOONS VIRGIN OLIVE OIL, PLUS EXTRA FOR THE DISH

PEPPER

Cook the onions in their skins in boiling salted water for 15 minutes. Drain then run cold water over them. When cool enough to handle, cut off and reserve the top quarter or so of each onion. Using a teaspoon or melon baller, carefully scoop out the center of the onions, leaving a shell 2-3 layers thick. Sit these upright in an oiled baking dish.

Finely chop the centers and mix with the cheese, sun-dried tomatoes, egg yolks, herbs and plenty of pepper. Divide between the onion shells, replace the reserved tops, trickle over the olive oil and bake in a preheated oven, 350°F, for 30-40 minutes, basting with the cooking juices towards the end. Serve warm or cold.

Serves 4 as first course, 2 as a main course

Variation

Substitute 8 pitted and chopped oil-cured black olives for the sun-dried tomatoes.

MUSHROOMS WITH TOMATOES AND ANCHOVY

Small amounts of anchovy fillets imbue foods with a subtle savory flavor without imparting a detectable fishy taste, a trick canny Italians learned long ago. They also learned that it is a particularly effective way to enhance the taste of one of their most favorite foods, mushrooms.

4 TABLESPOONS OLIVE OIL

1 LARGE CLOVE OF GARLIC, FINELY CHOPPED

1 LB MEDIUM CAP MUSHROOMS, PREFERABLY CREMINI, HALVED

2 SUN-RIPENED TOMATOES, SKINNED, DESEEDED AND CHOPPED

4 ANCHOVY FILLETS, RINSED IF NECESSARY, CHOPPED

2 TABLESPOONS CHOPPED PARSLEY

SALT AND PEPPER

Heat the oil in a frying pan, add the garlic and cook for 1 minute. Add the mushrooms and cook, stirring occasionally, for 10-15 minutes until the juices evaporate and the mushrooms are beginning to brown.

Stir in the tomatoes, anchovies, 1 tablespoon of the parsley and salt and pepper. Simmer for 5 minutes until lightly thickened.

Transfer to a serving dish and sprinkle with the remaining chopped parsley.

Serves 4

GENOESE MUSHROOMS AND POTATOES

This Ligurian recipe for potatoes with mushrooms is a clever way of making it appear as if there are more mushrooms than there are because the potatoes absorb the flavor of the mushrooms. The characteristic Ligurian touch of adding basil gives a final fillip to the dish. The mushrooms should really be fresh porcini (ceps), but as these are rarely available, I boost cultivated mushrooms, preferably cremini, with dried ceps.

1½ TABLESPOONS DRIED CEPS

1¼ CUPS HOT WATER

12 OZ MUSHROOMS, THINLY SLICED

3 MEDIUM POTATOES, THINLY SLICED

4 CLOVES OF GARLIC, CRUSHED

LEAVES FROM A BUNCH OF BASIL

OLIVE OIL

SALT AND PEPPER

Soak the dried mushrooms in the hot water for 30 minutes. Drain off and strain the liquid through cheesecloth or a filter paper. Simmer the reconstituted mushrooms in the liquid until the liquid has evaporated. Toss with the fresh mushrooms, potatoes, garlic, basil and seasoning.

Oil a baking dish that will hold the potatoes and mushrooms in a layer no more than about 1½ inches deep. Make an even layer of the mushroom mixture and bake in a preheated oven, 350°F, for about 45 minutes until the potatoes are tender; turn the ingredients over about halfway through the cooking time. Let stand for a couple of minutes before serving.

Serves 4

TURKISH STUFFED EGGPLANT

Stuffed eggplant is frequently called "Immam bayeldi," which, in Turkish, means "the sultan (or priest) fainted," supposedly at the amount of oil used in its making, but whether his swoon was from delight at the quality of the dish or horror at its cost is not known. I have seen so many different versions that I have no idea what the recipe the sultan ate was like, although to be in line with the legend, oil should be used lavishly. In this recipe it is not but you can add more oil if you like. A modification I like is to add a topping of crumbled feta cheese and bread crumbs.

2 LARGE EGGPLANTS

2 TABLESPOONS OLIVE OIL

1 LARGE ONION, FINELY CHOPPED

2-3 CLOVES OF GARLIC, CRUSHED

1 SWEET RED PEPPER, CORED, DESEEDED AND CHOPPED

2 EXTRA LARGE SUN-RIPENED TOMATOES, SKINNED,

DESEEDED AND CHOPPED

2 TABLESPOONS CHOPPED PARSLEY

PINCH OF SUGAR (OPTIONAL)

SALT AND PEPPER

CHOPPED PARSLEY TO GARNISH

Cut the eggplants in half lengthways and scoop out most of the filling, leaving a thin wall. Chop the eggplant flesh, put in a colander, sprinkle with salt and leave for 30-60 minutes. Sprinkle salt inside the eggplant shells and leave upside down for 30-60 minutes. Rinse the eggplant shells and flesh, and dry well.

Heat the oil in a saucepan, add the onion and garlic and cook, stirring occasionally, until softened. Stir in the eggplant flesh and red pepper, cook for 2-3 minutes, then stir in the tomatoes, parsley and seasoning. Bring to a boil and simmer for 15 minutes, stirring occasionally, until lightly thickened. Adjust the seasoning and add a pinch of sugar, if necessary.

Place the eggplant shells, skin side down, in a sauté pan, deep-frying pan or lightly oiled shallow baking dish. Divide the filling between the shells and pour 2-3 tablespoons water around them to cover the base of the pan or dish. Cover and cook gently on top of the stove, or in a preheated oven, 400°F, for about 30 minutes until the eggplants are tender, and the cooking juices have evaporated. Sprinkle with parsley and cool a little before eating.

Serves 4

Fish & Seafood

Mediterraneans love fish and around the region you can eat some of the best fish in the world. Its freshness alone is truly memorable and is enhanced by simple cooking. The most popular method is broiling, preferably over an open fire, with fresh herbs or spices added, and a sharp-tasting ingredient, such as lemon or lime juice, tomatoes, capers or olives, to highlight the wonderful flavor of the fish.

RED MULLET IN VINE LEAVES

There is a dichotomy of opinion as to whether the scales of barbecued red mullet should be left on. If they are, they coalesce in the fierce heat of the fire to form a protective crust that keeps the flesh moist and tender; also the sea salt they contain will be concentrated, intensifying the tangy, sea-fresh flavor. The skin must, of course, then be removed before the fish is eaten. Others prefer to scale the fish before cooking to allow the flesh to be impregnated by the delicious flavor of the fire. It is often said that red mullet should be cooked like woodcock, with the liver still in situ to impart a gamey flavor to the flesh, but most red mullet on sale nowadays (which has probably been frozen even if sold "fresh") is pre-gutted.

2 LARGE, SUN-RIPENED TOMATOES, SKINNED, DESEEDED AND CHOPPED

2 CLOVES OF GARLIC, FINELY CRUSHED

4 ANCHOVY FILLETS, CHOPPED

4 TABLESPOONS CHOPPED PARSLEY

2 TABLESPOONS CHOPPED BASIL

12 VINE LEAVES

4 RED MULLET, EACH WEIGHING ABOUT ½ LB, SCALED AND RINSED

OLIVE OIL FOR BRUSHING

SALT AND PEPPER

TO GARNISH (OPTIONAL)

ANCHOVY FILLETS

BLACK OLIVES

Mix the tomatoes, garlic, anchovy fillets, parsley, basil and black pepper together with a fork.

Arrange 3 vine leaves slightly overlapping so they will fit under one fish. Spread one quarter of the tomato mixture over the leaf in the center, then place one fish on the leaves. Fold the leaves over the fish to form a parcel. Repeat with the remaining leaves, fish and tomato mixture.

Place the parcels in a single layer in a baking pan, brush with oil and bake in a preheated oven, 400°F, for 15 minutes. Carefully transfer to a warm serving plate and garnish with anchovy fillets and olives, if you like.

Serves 4

Overleaf:
From left to right: Red Mullet in Vine Leaves,
Tunisian Broiled Sardines and Fish Plaki

TUNISIAN BROILED SARDINES WITH TOMATO RELISH

With one of the richest and most diverse catches of fish in the Mediterranean, Tunisia has some delicious fish dishes.

16 FRESH SARDINES

SPRIGS OF CILANTRO TO GARNISH (OPTIONAL)

MARINADE

1 CLOVE OF GARLIC

2 TEASPOONS CORIANDER SEEDS, TOASTED

1 DRIED RED CHILE, DESEEDED AND CHOPPED

FINELY GRATED RIND AND JUICE OF 1 LIME

4 TABLESPOONS VIRGIN OLIVE OIL

SALT AND PEPPER

RELISH

4 SCALLIONS, WHITE PART ONLY, CHOPPED

JUICE OF 1 LIME

2 MEDIUM SUN-RIPENED TOMATOES, SKINNED, DESEEDED AND CHOPPED

1 HALF OF SUN-DRIED TOMATO, CHOPPED

½ DRIED RED CHILE, DESEEDED AND CHOPPED

3 TABLESPOONS CHOPPED CILANTRO

Using the back of a knife, de-scale the sardines. Cut off the fins with scissors and cut along the stomach. Remove and discard the intestines. Wash the fish thoroughly, pat dry with paper towels and lay in a shallow, non-metallic dish.

Using a pestle and mortar, pound the garlic, coriander seeds and chile together with a pinch of salt. Add the lime rind and juice, gradually work in the oil. Pour over the sardines, coat well with the mixture, cover and leave for about 1 hour, turning 2 or 3 times.

Blend the relish ingredients in a processor or blender. Cook the sardines under a broiler for 2-3 minutes each side, basting with marinade. Serve with the relish, and garnish with cilantro if you like.

Serves 4

Variation
Sardines with Lemon and Parsley – mix together 6 tablespoons olive oil, 3 tablespoons lemon juice, 2 tablespoons chopped parsley and salt and pepper. Brush the mixture over 2 lb prepared fresh sardines. Marinate for 1 hour, then cook fish under a preheated broiler for 2-3 minutes each side, brushing with the lemon mixture as the fish browns and when turning it. Serve with the remaining lemon mixture poured over, and lemon wedges.

FISH PLAKI

Plakis are a feature of both Turkish and Greek cuisines, but typically in Turkey the fish is cut into steaks or pieces and it may be served cold, whereas the fish in a Greek plaki is cooked whole. Lemon is also characteristic of the Greek version.

APPROXIMATELY 2½ LB FISH SUCH AS BREAM, STRIPED BASS,

GRAY MULLET, RED SNAPPER OR POMPANO, CLEANED AND SCALED

I LARGE LEMON

2 TABLESPOONS VIRGIN OLIVE OIL

I ONION, CHOPPED

I CARROT, FINELY CHOPPED

2 CLOVES OF GARLIC, CHOPPED

I TEASPOON CORIANDER SEEDS, CRUSHED

3 RIPE TOMATOES, SKINNED, DESEEDED AND CHOPPED

3 HALVES OF SUN-DRIED TOMATO, CHOPPED

⅓ CUP MEDIUM-BODIED DRY WHITE WINE

LEAVES FROM A BUNCH OF PARSLEY, FINELY CHOPPED

SALT AND PEPPER

Put the fish into a baking dish. Squeeze the juice from half the lemon and pour over the fish.

Heat the olive oil in a saucepan, add the onion and carrot and cook, stirring occasionally, until the onion has softened but not colored. Stir in the chopped garlic and cook for about 3 minutes.

Stir in the coriander seeds, tomatoes, sun-dried tomatoes, wine, parsley and salt and pepper and simmer for a few minutes until well blended. Using a spatula, lift the fish and pour about a quarter of the tomato mixture underneath. Lay the fish down again. Pour over the remaining tomato mixture. Thinly slice the remaining lemon half and lay the slices on top of the fish.

Cover the dish and bake in a preheated oven, 375°F, for about 40 minutes until the fish flakes when tested with the point of a sharp knife.

Serves 4

Variation

Cook sliced celery and/or sliced fennel with the onion and omit the coriander seeds.

SKATE WITH CAPER AND ANCHOVY SAUCE

Wild capers cling to apparently inhospitable rocky cracks and stone walls and in the Mediterranean in May, harvesters will have to comb the countryside gathering the buds as they burst into beautiful white or pink flowers with flowing purple stamens. Since caper bushes are usually scattered, pickers have to walk over ½ mile to collect 2 lb of buds. Even harvesting from cultivated bushes is back-breaking work. Although the vast majority of capers are preserved in vinegar, a few are packed in salt and these are well-worth snapping up if you see them; simply rinse off the salt before using. Spain is the world's largest producer of capers, with the majority grown in Andalusia, the Balearics and Murcia, where I tasted the most successful pairing of capers and local salted anchovies in a piquant sauce that really bought the skate to life.

I CLOVE OF GARLIC, CRUSHED

4 ANCHOVY FILLETS, RINSED IF NECESSARY

1¼ TEASPOONS MUSTARD

1½ TABLESPOONS CAPERS, RINSED

2 TABLESPOONS CHOPPED PARSLEY

I TABLESPOON CHOPPED TARRAGON

2 TABLESPOONS VIRGIN OLIVE OIL

4 TABLESPOONS LIME JUICE

2 TABLESPOONS OLIVE OIL

2 SKATE WINGS

SALT AND PEPPER

Crush the garlic with a pinch of salt using a pestle and mortar. Work in the anchovy fillets to make a paste, then mix in the mustard, capers, herbs, virgin olive oil, lime juice and pepper.

Heat the olive oil in a wide frying pan. Season the skate, using very little salt, add to the pan and fry over a high heat for 4-5 minutes each side, depending on the thickness.

Add the sauce and heat briefly to warm through.

Serves 2

TUNA WITH SUN-DRIED TOMATOES, OLIVES AND SAGE

Tuna fisheries have existed in the Mediterranean for centuries and have been of major commercial importance, but now they are declining, along with a reduction in the size of the catch. Sicily is one place where there are still a number and the tuna trap, the "tonnare," is a much-enjoyed ritual. This recipe is based on a dish served to me in Sicily by the cousin of an Italian friend. It has the typical impact of a southern dish, but unusually includes sage rather than chile.

1½ CUPS MEDIUM-BODIED DRY WHITE WINE

1½ CUPS FISH STOCK

10 OIL-CURED BLACK OLIVES, PITTED AND SOAKED

IN WARM WATER FOR 10 MINUTES

4 TABLESPOONS OLIVE OIL

4 FRESH TUNA STEAKS, ABOUT ½ LB EACH

1 SMALL ONION, FINELY CHOPPED

4 LARGE SUN-DRIED TOMATOES PACKED IN OIL,

DRAINED AND CUT INTO STRIPS

2 TEASPOONS FINELY CHOPPED SAGE

SQUEEZE OF LEMON JUICE

PEPPER

SAGE LEAVES TO GARNISH (OPTIONAL)

Boil the wine in a wide frying pan until reduced by half, then add the stock and boil until reduced to 1 cup. Meanwhile, drain and chop the olives.

Heat the oil in a heavy frying pan, add the tuna and cook until browned on both sides, but still pink in the center, about 4-5 minutes each side. Transfer to a warm plate, cover and keep warm. Add the onion to the frying pan and cook, stirring, for about 2 minutes. Stir in the reduced wine and stock, the tomatoes and chopped sage and bring to a boil, scraping the bottom of the pan to dislodge the sediment. Boil until the liquid is reduced to ¾ cup. Add the olives and lemon juice and pepper to taste. Pour over the fish and serve garnished with sage leaves, if you like.

Serves 4

SQUID WITH SWEET PEPPER AND LEMON

This recipe from Pescara shows the characteristic Calabrian predilection for dishes packed with punchy flavor. Use small squid that are fresh and not frozen; check when buying the squid, as fish and seafood in display cabinets that looks fresh is often thawed frozen fish. To prepare fresh squid, follow the instructions in Calabrian Stuffed Squid (see page 69).

1 LB CLEANED SQUID

3 TABLESPOONS OLIVE OIL

1 SWEET RED PEPPER, CORED, DESEEDED AND CHOPPED

2 CLOVES OF GARLIC, CHOPPED

1 DRIED RED CHILE, CRUMBLED

FINELY GRATED RIND OF 1 SMALL LEMON

3 TABLESPOONS LEMON JUICE

1 TABLESPOON CHOPPED PARSLEY

SALT AND PEPPER

TO SERVE

LEMON WEDGES

COUNTRY BREAD (SEE PAGE 113)

Chop the squid tentacles roughly, and cut the bodies into ¼-½ inch thick rings.

Heat the oil in a sauté pan or deep frying pan, add the red pepper, garlic, chile and lemon rind and cook fairly gently, stirring occasionally, for about 5 minutes. Increase the heat to moderately high, stir in the squid and sauté until it becomes opaque and just tender, about 1-1½ minutes. Transfer to a warmed serving dish, sprinkle over salt, pepper and lemon juice to taste, sprinkle with parsley and serve immediately with lemon wedges and Country Bread.

Serves 4

*Left: Tuna with Sun-dried
Tomatoes, Olives and Sage
Right: Squid with Pepper and Lemon*

BREAM IN COUSCOUS JACKET, WITH TOMATO AND MINT SALAD

Several varieties of sea-bream are found in the Mediterranean – dentex, bogue, gilthead (daurade) and black-banded, with the best eating usually considered to be the dentex and gilthead. Fortunately, both are becoming more readily available here. The crisp, nutty coating in this recipe keeps the breams' flesh beautifully succulent and traps in the flavor.

1 PLUMP CLOVE OF GARLIC, CRUSHED

1 TEASPOON LIME JUICE

1 TEASPOON WHITE WINE VINEGAR

5 TABLESPOONS OLIVE OIL

2 LARGE SUN-RIPENED TOMATOES, SKINNED, DESEEDED AND CHOPPED

¾ CUP MINT, CHOPPED

⅓ CUP FINE COUSCOUS

¼ CUP BLANCHED ALMONDS, FINELY CHOPPED

1 SCALLION, THINLY SLICED

4 SEA-BREAM EACH WEIGHING ABOUT ½ LB, CLEANED AND SCALED

1 EGG, BEATEN

SALT AND PEPPER

Stir together the garlic, lime juice, vinegar and half the olive oil. Season then pour over the tomatoes, add half the mint and gently toss together. Cover and refrigerate.

Mix together the couscous, almonds, scallion, the remaining mint, plenty of black pepper and a little salt.

Dip each fish in the egg, then coat evenly with the couscous mixture.

Heat the remaining olive oil in a large, preferably non-stick, frying pan. Add the fish in a single layer and fry for about 7 minutes each side until the flesh flakes when tested with the point of a knife. Serve immediately with the tomato and mint salad.

Serves 4

BAKED FISH WITH "HOT" TAHINI SAUCE

Baking fish under a coating of flavored tahini is a favorite Lebanese method. The rich sauce bastes and flavors the fish and keeps the flesh moist and succulent.

1 SNAPPER OR OTHER BAKING FISH, WEIGHING ABOUT 4 LB, CLEANED AND SCALED, HEAD AND TAIL LEFT ON

4-6 CLOVES OF GARLIC

4 TABLESPOONS FINELY CHOPPED CILANTRO

½ CUP OLIVE OIL

½ CUP LEMON JUICE

½ CUP WATER

1 CUP TAHINI

¼-½ TEASPOON HOT CHILE POWDER

1 TABLESPOON TOASTED PINE NUTS

SALT

TO GARNISH

LEMON WEDGES

CILANTRO SPRIGS

With the point of a sharp knife, cut 2 or 3 slashes in each side of the fish, then rub the fish, inside and out, with salt. Cover and refrigerate for 1-2 hours.

Meanwhile, pound the garlic with a pinch of salt then mix in the cilantro.

Wipe the fish dry. Heat the oil in a large frying pan, add the fish and cook over a high heat for about 3 minutes each side. Transfer the fish to a baking dish and sprinkle with 1½ tablespoons of the lemon juice.

Pour all but 2 tablespoons of the oil from the pan. Stir in the garlic mixture and fry quickly until crisp, but do not allow it to burn. Remove from the heat.

Gradually beat the water into the tahini – the mixture will thicken. Next, gradually beat in the remaining lemon juice, then stir in the garlic mixture and chile powder to taste.

Pour over the fish, covering it completely and bake in a preheated oven, 350°F, for about 30-35 minutes until the fish is cooked through and the sauce is bubbling. Scatter the pine nuts over the fish and serve garnished with lemon wedges and cilantro sprigs.

Serves 4

CALABRIAN STUFFED SQUID

*The Calabrian coastline meanders its way around the
"boot" of Italy for more than 100 miles (the longest of
Italy's regions), with small craggy bays and deep water on
the west contrasting with shallow waters and longer beaches
on the east. Yet, surprisingly, fishing does not play a very
large part in local life. Squid, however, is popular.*

2 LB SMALL WHOLE SQUID

2 TABLESPOONS OLIVE OIL

3 SCALLIONS , WHITE PART ONLY, FINELY CHOPPED

3 CLOVES OF GARLIC, CRUSHED

1 CUP DRAINED, COOKED SPINACH

2 TABLESPOONS CHOPPED PARSLEY

SALT AND PEPPER

To prepare the squid, hold the head just below the eyes,
gently pull it away from the body and discard the soft
innards that come away with it. Pull out and discard the fine,
flexible quill that is attached to the inside of the body pouch.
Cut the head from the tentacles just below the eyes and
discard. The tentacles are joined together – in the center is
a beak-like mouth, which can be removed by squeezing it
out. Slip your fingers under the skin covering the body and
peel it off. Cut the fins away from either side of the pouch.
Rinse the pouch and dry thoroughly. Chop the tentacles.

Heat 1 tablespoon of the oil in a frying pan, add the
scallions and garlic and cook, stirring occasionally, for
2-3 minutes. Stir in the chopped tentacles, cook for a further
2-3 minutes, then tip into a food processor or blender. Add
the spinach and seasoning and process for about 1½ minutes.

Divide the spinach mixture between the body pouches of
the squid, close the openings with wooden toothpicks and
place the squid close together in a single layer in a shallow
baking dish. Sprinkle over the remaining oil and bake in a
preheated oven, 350°F, for about 20 minutes, until the squid
is tender.

Remove the toothpicks and sprinkle with the parsley.
Serves 4

BAKED STUFFED SARDINES

*Dishes of stuffed sardines are popular in Italy, particularly
throughout the south. The stuffing is usually placed between
two flattened sardines, like a sandwich, which may either be
baked, or coated in egg and bread crumbs and deep-fried. A
little grated Pecorino Romano can be added to this stuffing
and sprinkled on the fish with the bread crumbs.
Serve 1 "sandwich" per person for an antipasto, 2 for a
main course.*

12 FRESH SARDINES

1 CLOVE OF GARLIC

1 TABLESPOON EACH CHOPPED PARSLEY, CHIVES, DILL AND ROSEMARY

2 SMALL SAGE LEAVES, CHOPPED

¼ CUP PINE NUTS, LIGHTLY TOASTED AND COARSELY CHOPPED

2 TABLESPOONS LIGHT VIRGIN OLIVE OIL

½ LEMON

SCANT ½ CUP FRESH BREAD CRUMBS

SALT AND PEPPER

Cut the heads and tails from the sardines and slit along the
underside of the bodies to open them out. Discard the
intestines. Wash the cavities of the fish and pat dry with
paper towels. Lay one fish, skin-side uppermost, on a work
surface and press gently along the center of the back with
your thumbs to dislodge the backbone. Turn the fish over
and gently pull away the backbone. Repeat with the
remaining sardines.

Chop the garlic and herbs together finely, then mix with
the pine nuts, 1 tablespoon of the oil and seasoning.

Oil a wide shallow baking dish with a little of the
remaining oil and lay 6 of the sardines, skin-side down, in a
single layer in it. Squeeze over some lemon juice, then
spread some of the herb mixture on each fish. Cover with
the remaining sardines, skin-side up. Sprinkle with the bread
crumbs then trickle over the remaining oil. Bake in a
preheated oven, 425°F, for about 10 minutes, until golden.
Serve hot or at room temperature.
Serves 3

SHRIMP WITH FETA

If you are in Tourkalimenos in Piraeus, you will find this dish in all the restaurants. It may either be baked in an earthenware dish so the cheese is lightly browned or cooked on top of the stove. Traditionally, the shrimp shells are left on, which means eating them is not the easiest of things, so if you prefer, remove the body shells before cooking, leaving just the heads and tails in place.

3 TABLESPOONS OLIVE OIL

1 ONION, FINELY CHOPPED

2 CLOVES OF GARLIC, CRUSHED

4 OR 5 LARGE SUN-RIPENED TOMATOES, SKINNED, DESEEDED AND CHOPPED

3 TABLESPOONS CHOPPED PARSLEY

2 TEASPOONS DRIED OREGANO

⅓ CUP MEDIUM-BODIED DRY WHITE WINE (OPTIONAL)

2 LB RAW LARGE SHRIMP, IN THEIR SHELLS

½ CUP EWES' MILK FETA CHEESE

PEPPER

COARSELY CHOPPED PARSLEY TO GARNISH

Heat the oil in a flameproof earthenware casserole dish, add the onion and garlic and fry, stirring occasionally, until softened but not colored. Stir in the tomatoes, parsley, oregano and wine, if using and simmer until reduced and lightly thickened. Season with pepper only (the feta cheese will add salt).

Gently stir the shrimp into the sauce and simmer for 4-5 minutes. Crumble over the feta cheese and cook for a further 5 minutes. Serve garnished with the coarsely chopped parsley.

If cooking in the oven, bake in a preheated oven, 350°F, for 15 minutes.

Serves 4

GOLDEN ESCABECHE

In the days before refrigeration and deep-freezing, when there was too much fish to be eaten immediately, it would be cooked, then steeped in an acid-based marinade to help extend its edible life and so save many a case of food poisoning; spices or herbs were often included to make dull fish more interesting. The name "escabèche" is derived from the Perso-Arabic word "sikbaj," which means "vinegar stew," and similar dishes for meat, poultry, game and vegetables, as well as fish, are found along the length of the Mediterranean shores.

6-8 FILLETS OF SEA BREAM, SCALED WITH THE SKIN LEFT ON

3 TABLESPOONS SEASONED WHITE FLOUR

3 TABLESPOONS VIRGIN OLIVE OIL

MARINADE

2 TABLESPOONS VIRGIN OLIVE OIL

2 RED ONIONS, THINLY SLICED

1½ TEASPOONS CUMIN SEEDS, LIGHTLY CRUSHED

½ TEASPOON DRIED RED CHILE FLAKES

2 SWEET RED PEPPERS, CORED, DESEEDED AND SLICED

LARGE PINCH OF SAFFRON STRANDS, CRUSHED AND SOAKED

IN 3 TABLESPOONS WATER

FINELY SHREDDED RIND AND JUICE OF 1 ORANGE

2-3 TABLESPOONS LEMON JUICE

SUGAR TO TASTE

SALT AND PEPPER

CHOPPED CILANTRO OR PARSLEY TO GARNISH

For the marinade, heat the oil, add the onions and cook for 2 minutes. Stir in the cumin seeds and chile flakes for about 45 seconds. Add the peppers and fry, stirring occasionally, until soft, then add the saffron and liquid, orange rind and juice and lemon juice. Bubble for a few minutes and add sugar and seasoning to taste. Let cool.

Coat the fish in the seasoned flour, then fry in the oil until browned and just cooked through, about 2-3 minutes each side. Using a spatula, transfer the fish to a shallow non-metallic dish, let cool, then pour over the cooled marinade. Cover, place in the refrigerator and leave the fish for 4-12 hours, turning carefully 2 or 3 times. Return to room temperature 30 minutes before serving garnished with cilantro or parsley.

Serves 4 as a main course, 6-8 as a first course

Clockwise from top: Shrimp with Feta,
Golden Escabeche and
Turkish Skewered Swordfish

TURKISH SKEWERED SWORDFISH

Traditionally, the best place to eat fish in Turkey is Istanbul and some of the best I've eaten there has been bought from the most unpretentious of places – the flotilla of boats bobbing at the Eminonu end of the Galata Bridge. Here, arms reach up from the boats offering strollers enticing packages and fragrant skewers which have been cooked over braziers and charcoal burners wedged precariously in the little craft.

1¼ LB SWORDFISH, CUT INTO APPROXIMATELY

1 x 1½ INCH CUBES

OIL FOR GREASING

LEMON WEDGES TO SERVE (OPTIONAL)

MARINADE

4 TABLESPOONS LEMON JUICE

4 TABLESPOONS OLIVE OIL

3 TABLESPOONS FINELY CHOPPED RED ONION

2 BAY LEAVES, TORN

1½ TEASPOONS PAPRIKA

SALT AND PEPPER

LEMON SAUCE

3 TABLESPOONS VIRGIN OLIVE OIL

3 TABLESPOONS LEMON JUICE

3 TABLESPOONS CHOPPED PARSLEY

SALT AND PEPPER

Mix together the marinade ingredients. Lay the cubes of swordfish in a single layer in a wide, shallow, non-metallic dish. Pour over the marinade, turn the swordfish so it is evenly coated, cover and leave in a cool place for 4-5 hours, turning the fish occasionally.

Mix together the lemon sauce ingredients and set aside. Oil a broiler rack.

Thread the fish onto 4 skewers and cook under a preheated broiler or over a hot barbecue for 4-5 minutes each side, basting frequently with the marinade. Serve with the lemon sauce and lemon wedges, if you like.

Serves 4

FISH TAGINE WITH CHERMOULA

Chermoula is the name given to a popular characterful Moroccan marinade that is frequently used with many different types of fish which are to be baked, fried or broiled. However, don't expect fish with chermoula always to taste more or less the same because almost every cook has their own version – parsley may take the place of cilantro, onion is sometimes added, chile may be more or less pronounced and the ratio of other spices will fluctuate.

1½ LB GRAY MULLET, BREAM OR MONKFISH FILLETS

3 TABLESPOONS OLIVE OIL

3 CLOVES OF GARLIC, CRUSHED

1½ TEASPOONS GROUND CUMIN

1 TEASPOON PAPRIKA

1 FRESH GREEN CHILE, FINELY CHOPPED

HANDFUL OF CILANTRO LEAVES, FINELY CHOPPED

4 TABLESPOONS LEMON JUICE

SALT

LEMON WEDGES TO SERVE

Place the fish fillets in a shallow non-metallic dish. Mix together the olive oil, garlic, ground cumin, paprika, green chile, chopped cilantro, lemon juice and salt and pour over the fish. Cover and leave in a cool place for 3-4 hours, turning occasionally.

Cook the fish fillets under a preheated broiler for about 4 minutes each side, basting with the cilantro mixture occasionally, until the flesh flakes when tested with the point of a sharp knife. Serve warm with lemon wedges.

Serves 4

MOROCCAN SHRIMP WITH SPICES

Whenever I cook this dish my mind flies back to a glorious evening, when I was sitting beneath a deep royal blue Tangier sky, the sleepy sounds of night drawing in and the exotic aroma of shrimp being cooked in this way wafting tantalizingly past my nose. The shrimp can also be butterflied (use scissors to cut the shrimp lengthways almost in half, leaving the tails intact), then marinated in the spice mixture before broiling for 3-4 minutes; brush with any remaining marinade during cooking.

1 LB RAW LARGE SHRIMP IN THEIR SHELLS

4 TABLESPOONS OLIVE OIL

2 CLOVES OF GARLIC, CRUSHED

1 TEASPOON GROUND CUMIN

½ TEASPOON GROUND GINGER

1 TEASPOON PAPRIKA

¼ TEASPOON CAYENNE PEPPER

LEAVES FROM A BUNCH OF CILANTRO, FINELY CHOPPED

SALT

LEMON WEDGES TO SERVE

Remove the shells, legs, heads and tails from the shrimp. Cut along the back with the point of a sharp knife and remove the dark thread.

Heat the olive oil in a frying pan, add the garlic and cook until it becomes aromatic. Stir in the cumin, ginger, paprika and cayenne pepper, heat for about 30 seconds, then add the shrimp. Fry quickly, stirring, until they turn pink. Stir in the cilantro, heat for about 30 seconds, then serve the shrimp with the cooking juices spooned over and accompanied by lemon wedges.

Serves 4

GRILLED BUTTERFLIED SHRIMP WITH ROMESCO SAUCE

Gambas and langostini are large shrimp suitable for this recipe. Nora peppers are sold by specialist Spanish food shops, but if unavailable use 1 large sweet red pepper, charred, skinned and deseeded, and 1-2 small dried red chiles, soaked for 20 minutes in cold water and drained.

12-16 RAW JUMBO SHRIMP IN THEIR SHELLS

3 TABLESPOONS OLIVE OIL

½ CLOVE OF GARLIC, FINELY CRUSHED

1½ TABLESPOONS LIME JUICE

SALT AND PEPPER

LEMON WEDGES TO SERVE

SAUCE

2 NORA PEPPERS, DESEEDED, SOAKED FOR 20 MINUTES IN COLD

WATER, DRAINED (SEE ABOVE)

4 PLUMP CLOVES OF GARLIC, BROILED AND SKINNED

1 CUP MIXED HAZELNUTS AND BLANCHED ALMONDS, TOASTED

SMALL HANDFUL OF PARSLEY

4 TABLESPOONS RED WINE VINEGAR

½ CUP OLIVE OIL

To make the sauce, pound the peppers, garlic, nuts, parsley and seasoning to a paste in a mortar or mix in a food processor or blender. Mix in the vinegar, then slowly pour in the oil; the mixture should be thick and almost smooth. Adjust the seasoning and add a little more vinegar if necessary. Transfer to a bowl, cover and refrigerate for at least 1 day, or up to 1 week; transfer to room temperature 2 hours before serving.

Remove the legs and heads from the shrimp. Using sharp scissors, cut each shrimp lengthways from the head end almost to the tail; leave the tail intact. Place in a shallow dish. Mix together the remaining ingredients, pour over the shrimp, turn to coat with the marinade, leave for 30 minutes.

Cook under a preheated broiler, brushing occasionally with any remaining marinade, until the shrimp have opened out (butterflied) and are bright pink, about 3 minutes. Just before the shrimp are ready, stir the sauce then serve with the shrimp, accompanied by lemon wedges.

Serves 4

Variation

Omit the parsley; reduce the almonds to ¼ cup or use ¼ cup browned hazelnuts and add ½ lb extra large tomatoes, charred, skinned and deseeded.

Meat & Poultry

Around the Mediterranean meat is at a premium, so it is highly respected and cooked in the most sympathetic and quality-enhancing ways – often "stretched" by the addition of beans, rice, pasta, fruit and vegetables. Climate and religion dictate that lamb is the most common type of meat. Chickens are kept by many households, and game is enormously popular – hunting is a favorite pastime for the men of the region – and a rabbit hutch or pigeoncote housing unsuspecting occupants is still a common sight.

CHICKEN TAGINE WITH OLIVES AND PRESERVED LEMONS

This is one of the best-known Moroccan dishes. It cannot be made with fresh lemons, or, if it is, it will be an entirely different dish. Lemons preserved in salt lose their sharpness and have a mellow flavor which is complemented by pinky-brown Moroccan olives. If you are unable to find Moroccan olives, substitute Greek Kalamatas.

2 TABLESPOONS OLIVE OIL

I SPANISH ONION, FINELY CHOPPED

3 CLOVES OF GARLIC

I TEASPOON GROUND GINGER

1½ TEASPOONS GROUND CINNAMON

LARGE PINCH OF SAFFRON THREADS, TOASTED AND CRUSHED

I CHICKEN WEIGHING ABOUT 3½ LB

3 CUPS CHICKEN STOCK OR WATER

¾ CUP GREENY-BROWN MOROCCAN OLIVES,

RINSED, AND SOAKED IF LIKED

I PRESERVED LEMON (SEE NOTE OPPOSITE), RINSED IF LIKED, CHOPPED

LARGE BUNCH OF CILANTRO, FINELY CHOPPED

LARGE BUNCH OF PARSLEY, FINELY CHOPPED

SALT AND PEPPER

COARSELY CHOPPED PARSLEY TO GARNISH

Heat the oil, add the onion and fry fairly gently, stirring frequently, until softened and a good golden color.

Meanwhile, in a mortar, crush the garlic with a pinch of salt, then work in the ginger, cinnamon, saffron and a little pepper. Stir into the onions, cook until fragrant, then remove from the pan and spread over the chicken. Put the chicken in a heavy saucepan or flameproof casserole dish that it just fits, add the stock or water and bring to just on simmering point. Cover and simmer very gently for about 1¼ hours, turning the chicken over 2 or 3 times.

Add remaining ingredients to the pan, cover again and cook for a further 15 minutes or so until the chicken is very tender. Taste the sauce – if the flavor needs to be more concentrated, transfer the chicken to a warm shallow serving dish, cover and keep warm, then boil the cooking juices to a rich sauce. Tilt the pan and skim off surplus fat, if you like, pour over the chicken and garnish with parsley.

Serves 4

Overleaf:
Clockwise from top right: Chicken Tagine
with Olives and Preserved Lemons,
Arni Frikase and Pork with Fennel

Note
Preserving Lemons

To preserve lemons, put 2 teaspoons of coarse salt in a scalded Mason jar. Holding a lemon over a plate to catch the juice and using a sharp, stainless steel knife, cut lengthways as if about to quarter it, but do not cut quite through – leave the pieces joined. Ease out any pips.

Pack 1 tablespoon of salt into the cuts, then close them and place in the jar. Repeat with more lemons, packing them tightly and pressing each layer down hard before adding the next layer, until the jar is full. Squeeze another lemon and pour the juice over the fruit. Sprinkle with more coarse salt and top up with boiling water to cover the lemons.

Close the jar tightly and keep in a warmish place for 3-4 weeks. Do not worry if, on longer storage, a lacy white film appears on top of the jar or on the lemons; it is quite harmless – simply rinse it off.

If you like, a mixture of 1 stick of cinnamon, 3 cloves, 6 crushed coriander seeds, 3 black peppercorns and 1 bay leaf can be layered with the lemons.

ARNI FRIKASE

Arni Frikase is simply a lamb casserole and may be flavored with one or more of a number of vegetables, such as carrots, celery, lettuce, peas, artichokes and celeriac. This version reminds me of a lunch I enjoyed on the island of Cos, when a similar recipe was served for everyone seated around the rough wooden tables outside the taverna. The only accompaniments were home-made bread to mop up the juices and wine to wash down the fragrant meal.

1¼ LB BONED SHOULDER OF LAMB, CUBED

1 ONION, THINLY SLICED

1 CARROT, THINLY SLICED

1 STICK OF CELERY, THINLY SLICED

BOUQUET GARNI INCLUDING OREGANO, SAVORY AND THYME

4-6 ARTICHOKES, TRIMMED (SEE PAGE 54)

1 CUP BABY ONIONS, PEELED, OR LARGE SCALLION BULBS

1 TIGHT ROMAINE LETTUCE, QUARTERED LENGTHWAYS

4 EGG YOLKS

3-4 TABLESPOONS LEMON JUICE

SALT AND PEPPER

CHOPPED DILL TO SERVE

Put the lamb, onion, carrot, celery, bouquet garni and seasoning in a heavy, flameproof casserole dish and add water to cover. Heat to just on simmering point, remove the scum from the surface, cover the casserole dish and cook very gently for about 30 minutes. Add the artichokes and baby onions, if using, and cook for a further 35 minutes or so, until the meat and artichokes are just about tender. If using scallion bulbs, add them 5 minutes before the end. Add the lettuce and cook for a further 5 minutes.

Using a slotted spoon, transfer the meat and vegetables to a warm serving dish, cover and keep warm. Discard the bouquet garni.

Tilt the casserole dish, spoon off the fat from the surface of the cooking liquid, then boil the liquid, if necessary, to make about 1¼ cups.

Stir the egg yolks with the lemon juice and the chopped dill, stir in a ladleful of the cooking liquid, then pour back into the casserole dish and heat gently, stirring, until it is lightly thickened. Lightly but thoroughly stir into the meat and the vegetables.

Serves 4

PORK WITH FENNEL

The lift and faint sweetness that the aniseed flavor of fennel gives to pork is further highlighted by the last minute addition of gremolada, an Italian mixture of finely grated lemon rind and finely chopped parsley and garlic.

APPROXIMATELY 2 LB LEAN PORK, CUT INTO LARGE CHUNKS

1 TEASPOON CHOPPED THYME

1 TEASPOON FENNEL SEEDS, CRUSHED

2 CLOVES OF GARLIC, CHOPPED

2 CUPS MEDIUM-BODIED DRY WHITE WINE

SEASONED ALL-PURPOSE FLOUR

3 TABLESPOONS EXTRA VIRGIN OLIVE OIL

½ CUP PANCETTA, CUT INTO THIN STRIPS

2 ONIONS, SLICED

2 FENNEL BULBS

SALT AND PEPPER

GREMOLADA

1½ TEASPOONS FINELY GRATED LEMON RIND

½ CLOVE OF GARLIC, FINELY CHOPPED

2 TABLESPOONS CHOPPED PARSLEY

FEATHERY FENNEL FRONDS, CHOPPED (SEE METHOD)

Put the pork into a non-metallic dish, sprinkle over the thyme, fennel seeds and garlic, then pour over the wine. Cover and leave to marinate in a cool place for 4-12 hours, turning the pork occasionally.

Lift the pork from the marinade, pat dry and coat lightly with seasoned flour. Heat 1 tablespoon of the oil in a heavy flameproof casserole dish, add the pancetta and cook until lightly browned and the fat runs. Transfer to paper towels. Add the pork to the casserole dish in batches and brown evenly. Transfer to paper towels to drain.

Add remaining oil and onions to the pan, fry gently 5-8 minutes until soft and beginning to brown. Pour in marinade, stirring to dislodge the sediment, and bring to the boil. Bubble for a couple of minutes, then return the pork and pancetta to the pan. Season, cover tightly and cook gently on the stove or in a preheated oven, 325°F, for 1 hour.

Trim and reserve the feathery fronds from the fennel bulbs, then cut each bulb into six wedges. Add to the casserole dish, cover again and cook for a further 30 minutes until the pork and fennel are tender. Mix together the gremolada ingredients and scatter over the casserole.

Serves 5-6

MOUSSAKA

*Moussaka is an Arabic name given to a Greek pie of
ground meat layered with vegetables, usually eggplant, then
covered by a white sauce. It derives from "muhklabah," a
medieval Arab dish made of rice and sometimes nuts as well
as eggplants and ground meat. It was taken through the
streets of country villages to be put in the baker's
oven to cook. Moussaka shares a number of features with
Baked Lasagne (see page 105) – both are layered and
include similar ground meat and béchamel sauces and
both are much abused. If you do not have time to leave
the milk to infuse, omit the carrot, onion and bay leaf
and, instead, flavor the sauce with a little freshly grated
nutmeg. The béchamel sauce can be made in advance and
left for a couple of hours in a cool place, with a sheet of
wax paper lying on the surface, or overnight in
the refrigerator. You may need to stir in a little milk
before using it, as it will thicken on standing.
Moussaka always tastes better if it is made a day in
advance and reheated.*

3 EGGPLANTS CUT INTO SLICES ABOUT ½ INCH THICK

I LARGE ONION, FINELY CHOPPED

3 CLOVES OF GARLIC, CRUSHED

OLIVE OIL FOR FRYING

1¼ LB LEAN LAMB, GROUND

4 SUN-RIPENED TOMATOES, CHOPPED

2 HALVES OF SUN-DRIED TOMATOES, CHOPPED

I TEASPOON GROUND CINNAMON

I TABLESPOON CHOPPED PARSLEY

½ CUP KEFALOTIRI OR PARMESAN CHEESE, GRATED

SALT AND PEPPER

BECHAMEL SAUCE

2½ CUPS MILK

¼ ONION

PIECE OF CARROT

SPRIG OF PARSLEY

I BAY LEAF

4 TABLESPOONS UNSALTED BUTTER

3 TABLESPOONS ALL-PURPOSE FLOUR

2 EGGS, BEATEN

SALT AND PEPPER

Sprinkle the eggplant slices generously with salt, put in a
colander and leave for 30-60 minutes. Rinse well and dry
with paper towels.

Meanwhile, fry the chopped onion and crushed garlic in a
little olive oil in a large frying pan, until lightly browned. Add
the ground lamb and cook until browned, stirring to break
up any lumps. Stir in the chopped tomatoes, sun-dried
tomatoes, cinnamon, chopped parsley and a little black
pepper and simmer gently for about 20 minutes, stirring
occasionally, until the sauce is thick.

To make the béchamel sauce, gently heat the milk in a
saucepan with the vegetables and herbs, until the milk
comes to a boil. Remove from the heat, then cover the pan,
leave for 15 minutes, then strain.

Melt the butter in a heavy-bottomed saucepan, gradually
stir in the flour and cook for about 30 seconds. Over a low
heat, slowly pour in the milk, stirring constantly, then bring
to the boil, stirring. Simmer for about 5 minutes, stirring
occasionally. Remove from the heat and stir in the beaten eggs
and seasoning to taste.

Heat a thin layer of oil in a large frying pan, add the
eggplant slices in batches and fry until golden on both sides.
Using a slotted spoon, transfer the eggplant slices to paper
towels to drain.

Layer the eggplant and meat mixture in a casserole dish,
ending with a layer of eggplant. Pour over the béchamel
sauce, sprinkle evenly with the grated cheese then bake,
uncovered, in a preheated oven, 350°F, for 45 minutes until
golden brown.

Serves 6

CHICKEN BREASTS WITH FRAGRANT HERB STUFFING

*Although fresh herbs are now available all year round,
I prefer to reserve a recipe like this — where their flavor
affects the quality — for summer cooking when the sun will
have given them more taste.*

1½ CUPS MIXED HERBS SUCH AS BASIL, THYME, MARJORAM AND PARSLEY

1 CLOVE OF GARLIC

3 TABLESPOONS SOFT CHEESE, SUCH AS RICOTTA

APPROXIMATELY 5 TABLESPOONS OLIVE OIL, PLUS EXTRA FOR BRUSHING

2 TABLESPOONS Parmesan CHEESE, FRESHLY GRATED

1 TABLESPOON PINE NUTS, CHOPPED

4 LARGE BONELESS CHICKEN BREASTS, SKINNED

4 TABLESPOONS MEDIUM-BODIED DRY WHITE WINE

SALT AND PEPPER

Pound the herbs, garlic and a pinch of salt together in a mortar with a pestle or chop finely using a mezzaluna, then transfer to a small bowl. Work in the soft cheese, then the oil. Lastly add the Parmesan cheese, pine nuts and pepper. If time allows, leave for 1-2 hours for the flavors to develop.

Place 1 chicken breast at a time between 2 sheets of plastic wrap, flatten slightly using a meat bat or rolling pin, then cut a deep pocket. Lay each breast on a piece of lightly oiled foil. Season lightly, spoon some herb paste into each pocket and seal with wooden toothpicks. Fold up the foil and spoon in 1 tablespoon of wine. Fold the foil over the chicken to form loose parcels, securing the edges tightly. Place on a baking sheet and cook in a preheated oven, 350°F, for 30-40 minutes, until the chicken is tender.

Serve the chicken warm with the cooking juices spooned over or let cool in the foil and serve sliced.

Serves 4

Variation
Chicken Breast Rolls with Tapenade – marinate the breasts in lemon juice and thyme for 8 hours. Beat out as above, spread with Tapenade (see page 23), then roll up and wrap in a slice of bacon, enclosing a sprig of thyme on one side and a bay leaf on the other. Cook as above.

PIGEON NICOISE

*It is well known that Frenchmen have a penchant for
shooting virtually anything that flies, so the pigeons that
raid their vineyards, fruit bushes and gardens are certainly
classed as fair game. The typically robust Provençal flavors
of this recipe will not be lost against the taste of wild birds,
and the red wine marinade will coax tough flesh into
mellowness. On the other side of the coin, it gives character
to young farm-reared birds and makes them taste more of
the wild.*

4 OVEN-READY YOUNG PIGEONS

2 ONIONS, SLICED

3 CLOVES OF GARLIC, CUT INTO THIN SLIVERS

½ BUNCH PARSLEY

2 CUPS RED WINE

⅓ CUP BRANDY

6 ANCHOVY FILLETS, SOAKED IF NECESSARY

¾ CUP PITTED Nicoise OLIVES

4 TABLESPOONS UNSALTED BUTTER

OLIVE OIL FOR BRUSHING

SALT AND PEPPER

PARSLEY LEAVES TO GARNISH

Put the pigeons in a single layer in a non-metallic dish. Scatter the onions, garlic and parsley over and around the birds. Pour over the wine and ¼ cup of the brandy. Cover and leave for several hours, turning the birds occasionally.

Meanwhile, using a pestle and mortar, pound the anchovy fillets with the remaining brandy, olives and butter. Add plenty of black pepper.

Lift the pigeons from the marinade, pat dry and brush with olive oil. Cook under a preheated broiler, basting frequently with the marinade, for 20-30 minutes until the skin is crisp and brown and the flesh still slightly pink. Leave in a warm place for 10-15 minutes, then halve each bird along the backbone and breast bone. Spread each half with the anchovy and olive mixture and serve immediately, garnished with parsley leaves.

Serves 4

SOUVLAKIA

The only time skewers of broiled cubes of lamb used to be found in Greece was during fiestas. Then, village cafés and stalls with "mangali," portable charcoal braziers, would cook them to order, threading individually specified quantities of lean and fat meat on long metal skewers, "souvles," cooking them, then placing in a split pita with a sprinkling of chopped onion and parsley. Now, they are almost ubiquitous throughout Greece.

1 TABLESPOON OREGANO

4 TABLESPOONS OLIVE OIL

2 TABLESPOONS LEMON JUICE

1¼ LB BONED LEG OF LAMB, CUT INTO CUBES

SALT AND PEPPER

TO GARNISH (OPTIONAL)

1 SPANISH ONION, QUARTERED THEN THINLY SLICED

LEMON WEDGES

Crush the oregano in a mortar with a pestle or in a bowl using the end of a rolling pin, then mix in the oil, lemon juice and pepper.

Thread the lamb onto small skewers. Lay the skewers in a shallow dish and pour over the oil mixture. Turn the skewers so the lamb is evenly coated and leave in a cool place for 1-1½ hours.

Broil the lamb skewers under a preheated broiler or over a barbecue fire, turning frequently, until the lamb is brown on the outside but still just pink inside, about 5-10 minutes. Sprinkle with salt and garnish with sliced onion and lemon wedges, if you like.

Serves 4

LAMB AND OKRA STEW

Middle Eastern dishes using okra are often simply called "bamia," the ethnic name for okra, no matter what the other ingredients. Small pods of okra are preferred and it is important when trimming off the conical cap not to pierce the inner seed pod, so allowing the sticky liquid it contains to seep out. Bamia without meat is often served hot or cold as a main course on fast days, but it also makes a good accompaniment to broiled or roasted meats or poultry.

3 TABLESPOONS VEGETABLE OIL

2 LB LEAN LAMB, CUBED

1 LARGE ONION, CHOPPED

3 CLOVES OF GARLIC

1 TEASPOON GROUND CORIANDER

½ TEASPOON GROUND CUMIN

1 LB OKRA, TRIMMED

4 SUN-RIPENED TOMATOES, SKINNED, DESEEDED AND CHOPPED

1-2 TABLESPOONS TOMATO PASTE

LEMON JUICE TO TASTE

SALT AND PEPPER

PARSLEY OR CILANTRO TO GARNISH

Heat the oil in a heavy flameproof casserole dish, add the lamb in batches and cook until brown. Using a slotted spoon, transfer the lamb to a bowl. Stir the onion and garlic into the casserole dish and cook, stirring occasionally, until lightly browned. Stir in the ground coriander and cumin, then add the okra. Cook for a few minutes more, stir in the tomatoes and tomato paste and enough lemon juice to taste; cook for a further 2-3 minutes.

Return the lamb to the casserole dish with any juices that have collected in the bowl. Add the seasonings and sufficient water almost to cover the lamb and bring to just simmering point. Cover tightly and cook gently for about 1½ hours until the lamb is very tender; gently stir occasionally during cooking and add a little warm water if necessary, but at the end of cooking the sauce should be thick. Serve sprinkled with parsley or cilantro.

Serves 4-6

Left: Souvlakia
Right: Lamb and Okra Stew

CHICKEN CASSEROLE WITH ALMONDS

Body is given to this lightly spiced Moroccan sauce by the finely chopped onion and almonds that are added at the beginning of the cooking so that they soften during the long, slow cooking.

1 LEMON, HALVED

4 CHICKEN QUARTERS

½ TEASPOON GROUND GINGER

½ TEASPOON GROUND CINNAMON

PINCH OF SAFFRON THREADS, TOASTED AND CRUSHED

1 SPANISH ONION, FINELY CHOPPED

1 CUP BLANCHED ALMONDS, CHOPPED

LEAVES FROM A LARGE BUNCH OF PARSLEY, FINELY CHOPPED

SALT AND PEPPER

Squeeze the lemon over the chicken, rub in the juice and season with salt and pepper. Mix together the ginger, cinnamon and saffron and spread over the chicken. Leave at room temperature for about 1 hour. Put the portions into a heavy flameproof casserole dish in which they just fit. Add the onion and almonds and sufficient water almost to cover.

Bring to just on simmering point, cover and simmer very gently for about 45-60 minutes, turning the chicken occasionally. Add the parsley and cook for a further 5 minutes.

Transfer the chicken to a warm plate, cover and keep warm. Boil the cooking juices to give a well-flavored sauce, adjusting the levels of the spices and seasonings, if necessary. Return the chicken to the casserole dish and turn in the sauce to coat.

Serves 4

AFELIA WITH PORK

Afelia is a Cypriot style of cooking vegetables or pork with coriander seeds and red wine and all dishes cooked in this way, irrespective of the main ingredient, are called simply "afelia." Cypriots are so fond of the taste of coriander seeds that the fragrant berries are a hallmark of the island's cooking. Adjust the level of coriander seeds according to your own taste.

1½ LB LEAN BONELESS SHOULDER OF PORK, CUBED

1 CUP FULL-BODIED RED WINE, OR MORE IF LIKED

1-2 TABLESPOONS CRUSHED CORIANDER SEEDS

4 TABLESPOONS OLIVE OIL

SALT AND PEPPER

FRESH CILANTRO SPRIGS TO GARNISH

Put the pork in an earthenware dish, pour over the wine and sprinkle with the coriander seeds and black pepper. Stir well, cover and leave in a cool place for 8-12 hours, turning the meat over occasionally.

Using a slotted spoon, remove the pork from the dish and dry on paper towels. Reserve the wine.

Heat the oil in a flameproof casserole dish, add the pork and fry, stirring occasionally, until evenly browned. Add the reserved wine and salt, bring to just below simmering point, cover tightly and cook very gently, stirring occasionally, for about 1 hour until the pork is very tender. Serve garnished with cilantro sprigs.

Serves 4

POT ROAST CHICKEN WITH LEMON AND ROSEMARY

When I ate this fairly standard Italian family chicken dish at the home of some friends near Amalfi, I was quite taken aback by the wonderful fragrant intensity of the lemon flavor. The local lemons were responsible, so I brought home a couple of dozen. I am now pleased to find that they are being imported into this country – they are larger than other lemons we get and have a fruitier fragrance.

2 TABLESPOONS OLIVE OIL

I TEASPOON UNSALTED BUTTER

I CHICKEN WEIGHING ABOUT 3½ LB, IN PIECES

2 CLOVES OF GARLIC, FINELY CRUSHED

½ CUP MEDIUM-BODIED DRY WHITE WINE

I SPRIG OF ROSEMARY

2 TABLESPOONS LEMON JUICE

PIECE OF LEMON RIND CUT INTO 5-6 FINE STRIPS

SALT AND PEPPER

Heat the oil and butter in a heavy, flameproof casserole dish. Add the chicken, skin-side down, and brown quickly and lightly, adding the garlic towards the end.

Stir in the wine, add the rosemary and seasoning, bubble for 2-3 minutes, then lower the heat, cover tightly and cook very gently for about 45-50 minutes, turning the chicken a couple of times, until the juices run clear.

Transfer the chicken to a warm serving plate, cover and keep warm in the oven with the heat turned off. Discard the rosemary then tilt the casserole dish and skim off most of the fat. Stir in the lemon juice to dislodge the sediment, add the strips of rind and bring to a boil over a high heat, stirring. Pour over the chicken.
Serves 4

STUFFED WHOLE ZUCCHINI

4 ZUCCHINI, ABOUT ⅓ LB EACH

I TABLESPOON OLIVE OIL

½ LB LEAN GROUND LAMB

½ TEASPOON GROUND ALLSPICE

I ONION, FINELY CHOPPED

I CLOVE OF GARLIC, CHOPPED

I TEASPOON CRUMBLED DRIED MINT

2 TABLESPOONS PINE NUTS, LIGHTLY TOASTED

I CUP GREEK EWES' MILK YOGURT

I TABLESPOON SESAME SEEDS, LIGHTLY TOASTED, TO GARNISH

Cut off and reserve the stem ends of the zucchini. Using an apple corer, hollow out the zucchini, taking care not to pierce the skins and leaving ¼ inch thick shells. Chop the scooped out flesh and reserve.

Heat the oil in a frying pan over a fairly high heat until hot but not smoking, add the ground lamb and allspice and cook, stirring, until the lamb is no longer pink. Using a slotted spoon, transfer to a strainer to drain. Pour off all but I tablespoon of fat from the pan. Add the onion to the pan and cook, stirring occasionally, until softened. Add the garlic and reserved zucchini flesh and cook, stirring occasionally, until pale golden. Stir in the cooked lamb, mint, pine nuts, 2 tablespoons yogurt and salt and pepper. Let cool.

Divide the meat mixture between the zucchini shells, replace the ends and secure with wooden toothpicks. Place in a steaming basket over a saucepan of simmering water, cover and steam for 20-25 minutes, until tender.

Meanwhile, warm the remaining yogurt to serve with the zucchini. The zucchini can either be served whole accompanied by the warm Greek yogurt sprinkled with sesame seeds, or cut into I inch thick slices, arranged on a large warm serving plate or individual plates, sprinkled with sesame seeds and a spoonful of yogurt added.
Serves 4

Variation

Stuffed Zucchini Boats – trim the ends from 4 medium-large zucchini, then halve lengthways. Using a teaspoon or melon baller, scrape out and discard all the seeds. Steam the zucchini halves for about 5 minutes, or until slightly relaxed. Arrange them as upright as possible in an oiled broiler pan. Mash together I cup ewes' milk feta cheese, 2 beaten eggs, approximately I½ tablespoons dill and season with pepper – no salt is required because of the saltiness of the cheese. Spoon the mixture into the zucchini and broil until well browned. Serve warm.

CIRCASSIAN CHICKEN

This classic Turkish recipe dates from the time of the Ottoman Empire in Turkey, when Circassian women captives in the Sultans' harems were renowned for their beauty and their culinary skills. The dish is garnished in characteristically Turkish fashion with walnut oil flavored with paprika. It is traditionally served lukewarm as a first course, but is also good cold, or hot if the chicken is reheated in the sauce. Unless all the nuts are absolutely fresh, cook another recipe instead.

1 CHICKEN, WEIGHING ABOUT 3½ LB

1 ONION, QUARTERED

1 CARROT, QUARTERED

1 BOUQUET GARNI

1½ CUPS SHELLED FRESH WALNUTS

2 SLICES CRUSTLESS COUNTRY BREAD (SEE PAGE 113)

1 CLOVE OF GARLIC, CRUSHED

2 TABLESPOONS WALNUT OIL

1 TEASPOON PAPRIKA

SALT AND PEPPER

CHOPPED PARSLEY TO GARNISH

Put the chicken into a saucepan in which it just fits, tuck the onion, carrot and bouquet garni around the bird, season and pour in sufficient water to come about two thirds of the way up the chicken. Bring to just boiling point, remove any scum, then cover and simmer very gently for about 1¼ hours, until the chicken is tender. Remove the chicken from the pan and leave until cool enough to handle. Boil the stock in the saucepan to reduce. Remove the skin and bones from the chicken and add them to the pan; slice the chicken flesh into neat portions and set aside.

Meanwhile, grind the fresh nuts with the bread in a blender. Add the garlic, then gradually add sufficient of the strained chicken stock (about 1 cup) to give a light creamy sauce. Mix half of the sauce with the chicken, pile on to a serving plate, then pour over the remaining sauce. Leave until lukewarm.

Just before serving mix the walnut oil with the paprika and trickle over the chicken. Garnish with a sprinkling of chopped parsley.

Serves 6 as a first course, 4 as a main course

KLEFTIKO

The name of this Cypriot dish originates from sheep rustlers who used to cook their meat in a sealed earthenware thick casserole dish, a "tava," buried in a fire so that the fragrant smells of the cooking would not waft into the air and give them away. To seal the lid, make a thick flour and water paste, roll it into a sausage and wrap around the join. Serve with plenty of lemon; a crisp green salad makes a good accompaniment.

1 SHOULDER OF LAMB, CUT INTO 4-6 PIECES OR 4-6 PIECES OF SHOULDER, WITH A TOTAL WEIGHT OF ABOUT ¾ LB, WELL TRIMMED

1 LARGE ONION, FINELY CHOPPED

2-3 CLOVES OF GARLIC, CHOPPED

4-5 TABLESPOONS LEMON JUICE

SEVERAL SPRIGS OF OREGANO

1 LARGE SPRIG OF ROSEMARY

2 BAY LEAVES

3 TABLESPOONS OLIVE OIL

SALT AND PEPPER

PLENTY OF LEMON WEDGES TO SERVE

Put the meat into a heavy, preferably earthenware, casserole dish then add the onion, garlic, lemon juice, herbs, oil, salt and pepper and sufficient water to come halfway up the lamb. Seal the lid in place with a flour and water paste and bake in a preheated oven, 325°F, for at least 2½ hours without removing the lid.

If possible, let the meat cool in the cooking liquid for several hours, preferably overnight, then gently but thoroughly heat through again the next day. Alternatively, check to see if the lamb is tender. When it is, pour off and reserve the cooking liquid and cook the meat, uncovered, at 400°F, until lightly browned, about 20 minutes. Serve with lemon wedges.

Serves 6

BROILED CHICKEN WITH CUCUMBER, YOGURT AND MINT SALAD

Around the Mediterranean, the preferred way to broil foods is in the centuries-old manner – over an open fire – as it gives a most appetizing flavor to the food. At an open-air party I was lucky enough to attend in the foothills of the Rif mountains, the flavor of broiled spices added another layer to the taste sensations. These in turn, were beautifully offset by the cool mixture of cucumber, yogurt and mint that appears throughout southern and eastern Mediterranean countries and is variously referred to as a sauce, salad or relish. In Turkey, it goes under the name of "cacik," in Greece "tzatziki."

The sauce can be omitted and the cooked chicken sprinkled with chopped cilantro.

4 CHICKEN PORTIONS

5 TABLESPOONS OLIVE OIL

2 CLOVES OF GARLIC, FINELY CRUSHED

1¼ TABLESPOONS PAPRIKA

1¼-1½ TEASPOONS GROUND CUMIN

SQUEEZE OF LEMON JUICE

PINCH OF CAYENNE PEPPER

SALT

SAUCE

½ CUCUMBER, PEELED AND HALVED LENGTHWAYS

¾ CUP GREEK EWES' MILK YOGURT

1 CLOVE OF GARLIC, CRUSHED

1-1½ TABLESPOONS CHOPPED MINT

SALT AND PEPPER

Put the chicken in a wide shallow dish. Mix together the oil, garlic, paprika, cumin, lemon juice and cayenne, pour over the chicken, turn to coat, then cover and leave in a cool place for 2 hours, turning the chicken 2 or 3 times.

Meanwhile, make the sauce. Scoop out and discard the seeds from the cucumber. Chop the cucumber, sprinkle with salt and leave in a colander for 30-60 minutes to drain. Rinse the cucumber and dry well with paper towels. Mix together the yogurt, garlic, mint and pepper, then stir in the chopped cucumber, pour into a serving bowl, cover and leave in the refrigerator.

Sprinkle salt over the skin side of the chicken and place under a preheated broiler for 8-10 minutes, until the skin is golden, brushing with the oil mixture remaining in the dish.

Turn the chicken over, sprinkle with salt and brush with the cooking juices and remaining oil mixture. Cook for a further 10 minutes or so until the juices run clear when the thigh is pierced with a sharp knife. Serve with the cucumber sauce.
Serves 4

Variation

Broiled Chicken with Herb and Lemon Marinade – place 4 chicken breasts in a single layer in a shallow non-metallic baking dish. Mix together the grated rind and juice of 1 lemon, 1 tablespoon olive oil, the finely chopped white and 1 inch green part of 2 scallions, 1 tablespoon chopped fresh thyme, 1½ tablespoons chopped cilantro, ¼ teaspoon ground coriander, salt and pepper. Pour the marinade over the chicken, cover and refrigerate for 8 hours, turning occasionally. Broil as above, basting occasionally. Serve garnished with cilantro sprigs.

CHICKEN WITH SAGE AND LEMON

A title this simple is not the sort to lead a prospective diner to expect anything out of the ordinary. But how wrong I was when I ordered this in Florence. The dish that arrived was a perfect example of how simplicity can be delicious.

4 BONELESS CHICKEN BREASTS, SKINNED

5 TABLESPOONS VIRGIN OLIVE OIL

3 TABLESPOONS LEMON JUICE

28 SMALL SAGE LEAVES

I TABLESPOON UNSALTED BUTTER

SALT AND PEPPER

2 LEMONS, HALVED, TO SERVE

Place the chicken breasts in a single layer in a non-metallic dish. Pour over 3 tablespoons of the oil and the lemon juice. Scatter over the sage leaves, turn the chicken so that the breasts are evenly coated, then cover and leave for about 30 minutes.

Lift the chicken breasts from the marinade and pat dry. Strain the marinade into a small bowl; reserve the sage leaves separately.

Heat the butter and remaining oil in a frying pan, add the chicken, smooth side down, and cook for about 5 minutes, until browned. Turn the chicken, season and tuck the sage leaves around. Cook for another 5 minutes or so until the underside is brown and the chicken cooked.

Transfer the chicken to a warmed serving plate, place the sage leaves on the chicken, cover and keep warm.

Tilt the pan and pour off the fat. Place the pan over the heat and stir in the reserved marinade, dislodging the sediment. Boil until reduced to a brown glaze, then pour over the chicken. Serve with the lemon halves.

Serves 4

Variation
Chicken with Sage and Ham – brown 4 chicken pieces in butter and oil in a large frying pan. Add ¼ cup chopped prosciutto, heat for I minute, stir in I cup medium-bodied dry white wine, bubble for I minute, then lower the heat. Add I tablespoon small sage leaves and seasoning, cover and simmer very gently for 45 minutes. Transfer the chicken to a warmed plate, cover and keep warm. Boil the cooking juices, scraping up the sediment, until lightly thickened. Add a squeeze of lemon juice, then pour over the chicken.

COUSCOUS

This is a favorite North African dish, ideal for an informal meal.

I LB LEAN LAMB, CUT INTO LARGE CUBES

2 ONIONS, QUARTERED THEN THICKLY SLICED

2 CLOVES OF GARLIC, CRUSHED

PINCH OF SAFFRON THREADS, CRUSHED

I TEASPOON GROUND CINNAMON

½ TEASPOON PAPRIKA

I FRESH RED CHILE, DESEEDED AND FINELY CHOPPED

½ TEASPOON GROUND GINGER

6 SMALL CARROTS, QUARTERED LENGTHWAYS

3 SMALL TURNIPS, QUARTERED

½ LB KOHLRABI OR CELERIAC, CUT INTO LARGE CHUNKS

4 CUPS PRE-COOKED COUSCOUS

2 TEASPOONS OLIVE OIL

2 SMALL ZUCCHINI, QUARTERED LENGTHWAYS

I½ CUP FAVA BEANS

4 TOMATOES, QUARTERED

LARGE BUNCH EACH PARSLEY AND CILANTRO, CHOPPED

I TABLESPOON UNSALTED BUTTER

SALT AND PEPPER

Put the lamb in a large saucepan. Add 3¾ cups water, the onion, garlic, spices and seasoning. Bring to a boil, remove the scum from the top, cover and simmer very gently for about 30 minutes. Add the carrots, turnips and kohlrabi or celeriac, cover again and simmer for 15 minutes.

Put the couscous into a large bowl, pour over about I¼ cups water, stir well and leave for 10 minutes. Add another I¼ cups water and the oil and fork through the couscous to make sure the grains are separate, then leave for 10 minutes until swollen and tender but still separate. Put into a steamer and place, uncovered, over a saucepan of boiling water for about 10 minutes.

Meanwhile, add the zucchini and fava beans to the lamb. Add the tomatoes and herbs and cook for a further 5 minutes until the vegetables and lamb are tender.

Fork through couscous to separate the grains, then turn onto a large serving plate. Dot the butter over the top, stir in and season. Form into a mound with a large well in the center, place lamb in the well. Using a slotted spoon, lift the vegetables from the cooking broth and place on and around the lamb. Serve remaining broth in a separate warm bowl.

Serves 4

PIGEON WITH KUMQUATS

In countries where red meat is limited, pigeons are a welcome addition to the diet, and so pigeoncotes are a common rural and urban sight in the Middle East. The birds are small and tender, more like Western farm-reared pigeons than wild ones. In addition, every year, hundreds of thousands of birds pass over the Mediterranean on their journeys to and from their summer and winter haunts. Each time, many hapless birds, especially quail and pigeons, fall victim to the hunters' guns – to end up in the cooking pot. If kumquats are not available, add 2 peeled and thickly sliced oranges when the cooking liquid is almost reduced.

3 TABLESPOONS OLIVE OIL

6 YOUNG OVEN-READY PIGEONS

½ LB BUTTON ONIONS, PEELED

I CINNAMON STICK

I BAY LEAF

¾-I TEASPOON GRATED FRESH GINGER ROOT

LARGE PINCH OF SAFFRON THREADS, TOASTED AND CRUSHED

3¾ CUPS CHICKEN STOCK

8 OUNCES KUMQUATS, HALVED

2 TABLESPOONS CLEAR HONEY

SALT AND PEPPER

LIGHTLY TOASTED ALMOND HALVES TO GARNISH

Heat the oil in a large, heavy flameproof casserole dish, add the pigeons in batches and cook until browned. Using a slotted spoon, transfer to a dish. Stir the onions into the casserole dish and sauté until golden. Stir in the cinnamon, bay leaf, ginger, saffron, stock and salt and pepper and bring to a boil.

Return the pigeons to the casserole dish with any juices that have collected in the dish, cover and cook gently, turning the pigeons occasionally, for about I hour, depending on their age, until becoming tender. Add the kumquats and honey, cover again and cook for a further 30-45 minutes until the pigeons are very tender. Using a slotted spoon, transfer the pigeons to a large warmed serving plate, cover and keep warm.

Boil the cooking liquid until lightly thickened. Discard the cinnamon and bay leaf, if you like. Pour the liquid over the pigeons and scatter over the almonds.
Serves 6

LAMB WITH ARTICHOKES

Lamb teamed with artichokes is a dish characteristic of southern Italian cooking. It combines vegetables with meat to make it go further; artichokes grow there in abundance and lamb is the meat most often eaten in a region where meat does not usually form part of the daily diet.

3 TABLESPOONS OLIVE OIL

I¼ LB YOUNG LAMB, CUT INTO I INCH CUBES

¼ CUP PROSCIUTTO, CUT INTO STRIPS

I BUNCH OF SCALLIONS, WHITE PART ONLY, CHOPPED

4 ARTICHOKES, TRIMMED (SEE PAGE 54)

¾ CUP VEAL STOCK

SALT AND PEPPER

CHOPPED MINT TO GARNISH

Heat the oil in a heavy-bottomed flameproof casserole dish, add the lamb and cook until evenly browned. Transfer to a warm bowl and keep warm. Stir the prosciutto and scallions into the casserole. Fry for about 30 seconds, then stir in the artichokes. Cook, stirring, for 5 minutes. Stir in the stock and return the lamb to the pan. Cook gently for about I5 minutes until the lamb and artichokes are tender. Add the seasoning and sprinkle with chopped mint.
Serves 4

Variation
Substitute artichokes that have been preserved in oil, adding them about 5 minutes before the lamb is ready, so they heat through; the oil from the artichokes can be used instead of olive oil for frying.

LAMB AND DRIED APRICOT TAGINE

"Tagine" is the Moroccan name both for a casserole or stew and the shallow earthenware pot in which it is cooked. Meat and fruit, fresh or dried, are frequent partners in southern Mediterranean dishes. Moroccans have a sweet tooth and add honey, sugar or both to their tagines. However, I have not done so for this recipe as I think the dried apricots provide sufficient sweetness to give a well-balanced taste.

3-4 TABLESPOONS OLIVE OIL

1¼ LB LEAN LAMB, CUBED

1 SPANISH ONION, FINELY CHOPPED

3 CLOVES OF GARLIC, CHOPPED

2 TABLESPOONS FRESH GINGER ROOT, PEELED AND FINELY CHOPPED

2 STICKS OF CELERY, THINLY SLICED

PINCH OF SAFFRON THREADS, TOASTED AND CRUSHED

1 TEASPOON CORIANDER SEEDS, TOASTED AND CRUSHED

1 TEASPOON CUMIN SEEDS, TOASTED AND CRUSHED

1 CUP DRIED APRICOTS, SOAKED OVERNIGHT JUST COVERED BY WATER

JUICE OF 1 ORANGE

SALT AND PEPPER

PARSLEY TO GARNISH

Heat the oil in a heavy flameproof casserole dish, add the lamb and cook until evenly browned. Transfer to a bowl. Stir the onion into the casserole and cook over a fairly low heat, stirring occasionally, until soft and the onion is beginning to color. Stir in the garlic and ginger, increase the heat to moderate and cook for about 1 minute. Stir in the celery, saffron, coriander and cumin for 30 seconds, then return the lamb and any juices to the casserole dish. Add salt and pepper and sufficient water just to cover the meat, cover the casserole dish tightly and cook gently for about 1 hour, stirring occasionally.

Stir the apricots and their soaking liquid, and the orange juice into the lamb, cover again and cook for a further 30 minutes or so until all the ingredients are tender and the liquid is reduced and well flavored. If there is too much liquid or it is too thin, transfer the meat and vegetables to a warmed serving dish and boil the liquid to concentrate it. Pour into the serving dish and stir the ingredients together. Garnish with parsley.

Serves 4

DAUBE PROVENCAL

The south of France does not always bask in sun. Wintertime in the Provençal and Languedoc hills can be decidedly chilly, calling for a large, slowly simmering pot of wine-laced daube. This daube oozes with the region's flavors – herbs, olives and anchovies. The characteristic flavor and texture result from cooking in a plump earthenware daubière nestled in the fire (see page 11). A daube is much better if it is prepared a day in advance so the flavors can mingle and mellow. The meat can also be marinated in the wine with the herbs if you like. Serve with noodles and a crisp green salad.

½ LB LEAN SALT PORK OR BACON, DICED

2½ LB LEAN CHUCK STEAK, CUT INTO 2 INCH CUBES

1 LARGE ONION, CHOPPED

3 CLOVES OF GARLIC, CRUSHED

3 CARROTS, FINELY CHOPPED

3 TOMATOES, CHOPPED

SPRIG EACH OF THYME, MARJORAM, ROSEMARY AND PARSLEY

2 BAY LEAVES

STRIP OF SUN OR OVEN-DRIED ORANGE RIND

2 ANCHOVY FILLETS, SOAKED IF NECESSARY, CHOPPED

6 BLACK PEPPERCORNS, CRUSHED

2¼ CUPS RED WINE

12 NICOISE OLIVES

SALT (OPTIONAL)

Gently cook the pork or bacon in a heavy frying pan until the fat runs. Add the beef in batches and fry, stirring frequently, until browned. Using a slotted spoon, transfer the meat when cooked to a heavy flameproof casserole dish.

Stir the onion into the frying pan and cook, stirring frequently, until softened and browned. Stir in the garlic towards the end. Stir in the carrots, tomatoes, herbs, orange rind, anchovies, peppercorns and wine to dislodge the sediment. Bring to a boil, pour over the meat, cover tightly and cook in a preheated oven, 325°F, for about 3½ hours until the meat is meltingly tender. Add the olives 10 minutes before serving. If there is too much liquid or it is too thin, remove the meat and keep warm and boil the cooking liquid to concentrate it. Stir the meat back into the casserole and add salt, if necessary.

Serves 6

Top: Lamb and Dried Apricot Tagine
Bottom: Daube Provençal

POACHED CHICKEN WITH LEMON SAUCE

It seems that every Greek garden, at least out in the country, has a lemon tree because Greeks love the flavor of lemon. It is present in innumerable dishes and is one of the pair of ingredients (the other is egg yolk) that comprise the classic Greek sauce thickener; the sauces themselves then being called Avgolemono (see page 17). In this recipe, the light, sharp lemony sauce poured over delicate, moist chicken makes a delicious and fresh-tasting dish.

3 LEMONS

1 CHICKEN WEIGHING APPROXIMATELY 3½ LB, IN PIECES

3 TABLESPOONS OLIVE OIL

APPROXIMATELY 3¾ CUPS CHICKEN STOCK

3 EGG YOLKS

½ CUP SOUR CREAM

SALT AND PEPPER

Cut one of the lemons in half and rub over the chicken. If there is time, leave at room temperature for about 1 hour.

Fry the chicken portions in the oil until browned, then transfer to a heavy, wide, flameproof casserole dish. Pour over sufficient stock just to cover the chicken. Add salt and pepper, bring to just simmering point, cover tightly and poach for 35-45 minutes until the chicken is very tender. Remove the chicken from the dish. Increase the heat beneath the casserole dish and boil the stock until reduced to about 1¼ cups.

Meanwhile, skin the chicken and remove the flesh from the bones in large pieces. Add skin and bones to the stock and place chicken on a warm dish. Cover and keep warm.

Squeeze the remaining lemons. Blend the egg yolks with 5 tablespoons of lemon juice, then stir in the sour cream. Discard the skin and bones from the stock, then tilt the casserole dish and skim any fat from the surface. Lower the heat. Stir a few spoonfuls of the stock into the egg yolk mixture, then pour into the casserole dish. Cook, stirring, until lightly thickened, but do not allow to boil. Adjust the level of lemon juice and seasonings, if necessary. Pour some sauce over the chicken and serve the rest separately in a warmed pitcher.

To serve cold, place the cooked chicken as it is removed from the bones on a large cold plate and let cool. Let the sauce cool, stirring frequently, then spoon it over the chicken pieces.

Serves 4

VEAL WITH SAGE AND PROSCIUTTO

Although nearly every Italian restaurant has several veal dishes on the menu, historically, veal was not used south of Tuscany, with the exception of the Roman speciality, Saltimbocca (see below). Using the same ingredients as Saltimbocca – veal, prosciutto, sage – this recipe is based on one I ate at Arancio d'Oro, a small trattoria in Rome.

1 TABLESPOON UNSALTED BUTTER

2 TABLESPOONS OLIVE OIL

4 LARGE VEAL CHOPS

¾ CUP MEDIUM-BODIED DRY WHITE WINE

10 SMALL-MEDIUM SAGE LEAVES, COARSELY CHOPPED

2 SLICES OF PROSCIUTTO, FINELY CHOPPED

VEAL STOCK OR WATER (OPTIONAL)

PEPPER

LEMON WEDGES TO SERVE

Heat the butter and oil in a large, heavy frying pan over a moderate heat. Add the veal and cook until golden brown on both sides, about 5 minutes. Add the wine, bubble gently until almost evaporated, then add the sage and prosciutto. Lower the heat and cook gently for about 10 minutes, turning the veal once, until cooked through. Stir in stock or water, if necessary to prevent the veal becoming dry. Season with pepper then transfer the veal to a serving plate. Stir the juices to dislodge the sediment, adding stock or water if necessary, then pour over the veal. Serve with lemon wedges to squeeze over the veal.

Serves 4

Variations

Veal with Lemon, Capers and Parsley – coat 2 veal cutlets in seasoned flour, then fry briskly in 2 tablespoons olive oil for about 1 minute each side. Transfer to warmed plates, cover and keep warm. Add 2 tablespoons each lemon juice and chopped parsley and 1 tablespoon capers, then whisk in 1 tablespoon diced unsalted butter until the butter melts. Season and pour over the veal. **Serves 2**

Saltimbocca – lay a slice of prosciutto on each of 4 veal cutlets, scatter 2 shredded small sage leaves over each slice then roll up and secure with wooden toothpicks. Fry in a little olive oil and unsalted butter, until browned, then pour over about ½ cup medium-bodied dry white wine, allow to bubble for about 1 minute. Season with pepper and serve with lemon wedges. **Serves 4**

CHICKEN WITH GARLIC AND OREGANO

Oregano is a wild form of marjoram and the flavor can vary with the soil and climate; Greek oregano usually has a more robust flavor and so will withstand long, slow cooking. (Incidentally, rigani is the collective Greek name for a number of wild varieties of oregano and is not available fresh commercially.) Don't be put off by the amount of garlic used in this recipe or reduce it. During the long slow cooking, it mellows as it softens.

1 CHICKEN WEIGHING ABOUT 3½ LB

1 LEMON

2-3 BULBS OF GARLIC, DIVIDED INTO CLOVES WITHOUT PEELING

1 BUNCH OF OREGANO, DRIED, PREFERABLY IN A SUNNY WINDOW,

FOR A FEW HOURS

1 CUP MEDIUM-BODIED DRY WHITE WINE

SALT AND PEPPER

Season the chicken inside and out. Thoroughly prick the lemon all over with a needle and put it inside the chicken. Put some of the garlic cloves and some of the oregano on the base of a heavy, deep, flameproof casserole dish in which the chicken will fit with just a little room to spare. Put the chicken into the casserole dish and tuck the remaining oregano and garlic around it. Pour over the wine and cover the casserole with wax paper followed by a lid. Cook in a preheated oven, 400°F, for 30 minutes, then lower the oven temperature to 350°F, and cook for a further 1¼-1½ hours until the chicken is very tender.

Lift the chicken from the casserole dish and tip the juices from the cavity into the casserole dish. Place the chicken on a warmed serving dish and keep warm.

Discard the oregano from the casserole dish and remove and reserve the garlic. Tilt the casserole dish and spoon off the fat from the surface of the juices, then boil them to reduce to taste. Return the garlic to the sauce, then pour it into a warm gravy boat to serve with the chicken.

Serves 4

Variations

Quick Chicken with Garlic – boil garlic cloves in 3 separate changes of water. Purée the cloves and insert between the skin and flesh of chicken before broiling.

Chicken with Aïoli – either spread Aïoli (see page 24) between the flesh and skin of chicken portions before broiling, or serve Aïoli with the chicken.

VIBRANT DUCK WITH ORANGES AND OLIVES

This dish is a combination of Catalan and Valencian influences – Barbary-type duck from Catalonia and fruit from the lush groves of Valencia. Traditionally, a whole duck would be used, but I prefer to use duck breasts or portions, as they are more economical, produce less fat and are easier to serve. The fat removed from the duck before cooking is very good for frying, particularly potatoes and mushrooms; it just needs to be rendered down first.

4 DUCK BREASTS, EACH WEIGHING ⅓ LB

3 ORANGES

1 LEMON

2 TABLESPOONS OLIVE OIL

1 ONION, CHOPPED

3 CLOVES OF GARLIC, CRUSHED

¼ CUP RAW COUNTRY HAM, CHOPPED

2 TABLESPOONS BRANDY

¾ CUP MEDIUM-BODIED DRY WHITE WINE

1 CUP CHICKEN STOCK

12 WHOLE BLACK OLIVES

SALT AND PEPPER

SPRIGS OF TARRAGON TO GARNISH

Remove the duck skin and excess fat. Cut the skin and pith from the oranges and lemon and slice the fruit thinly.

Heat the oil in a heavy flameproof casserole dish, add the duck breasts, two at a time, and fry until browned. Transfer to paper towels to drain. Stir the onion and garlic into the casserole dish and cook over a medium heat, stirring occasionally, until softened and lightly browned. Stir in the ham, brandy, white wine and stock to dislodge the sediment then add all the lemon slices, three-quarters of the orange slices and the seasoning. Bring to a boil, bubble for a couple of minutes, then add the duck, turning the pieces over in the sauce. Cover and cook in a preheated oven, 350°F, for 50-60 minutes until the duck is quite tender.

Transfer the duck to a warmed serving plate, cover and keep warm in the oven with the heat turned off. Pass the cooking juices through a strainer into a saucepan, pressing down well on the fruit. Skim the fat from the surface of the liquid, then simmer until lightly thickened. Add the olives, adjust the seasoning and pour over the duck. Garnish with the remaining orange slices and tarragon.

Serves 4

Pasta, Beans & Grains

Beans and grains – and the products made from them, such as pasta – all feature prominently in the Mediterranean diet. Beans such as chick peas and lentils go into dips and casseroles. Rice, rarely served plainly boiled, is more often turned in hot oil, with herbs, spices, nuts and vegetables added later. Wheat is not only made into pasta, but also into couscous – a type of fine semolina particularly enjoyed in North Africa. Pasta is usually associated with Italy, but many other Mediterranean countries have their own versions, such as the fideos of Spain.

CHICK PEAS WITH SPINACH

This sustaining, simple, inexpensive and well-flavored recipe for a meal in a pot, exemplifies the type of dish that hungry, country-living Spanish families will tuck into during the winter. The original Spanish recipe included the traditional thickening of fried bread crushed with the garlic, but for the sake of lightness I leave it out.

1 HEAPING CUP CHICK PEAS, SOAKED OVERNIGHT, DRAINED AND RINSED

2½ TABLESPOONS OLIVE OIL

1 SPANISH ONION, FINELY CHOPPED

½ LB RAW CHORIZO, THICKLY SLICED (OPTIONAL)

2 LARGE SWEET RED PEPPERS, CORED, DESEEDED AND SLICED

1 TABLESPOON PAPRIKA

¼-½ TEASPOON CUMIN SEEDS, FINELY CRUSHED

1 LB SPINACH, CHOPPED

3 CLOVES OF GARLIC

SALT AND PEPPER

Cook the chick peas in 1½ times their volume of boiling water until tender, 1½-2 hours.

Meanwhile, heat 1½ tablespoons of the oil in a frying pan, add the onion and cook slowly, stirring occasionally, for 5 minutes. Add the chorizo, if using, and cook for a further 5-10 minutes until the onion is very soft. Stir in the red peppers and continue to cook, stirring occasionally, for about 10 minutes.

Heat the remaining oil in a saucepan, stir in the paprika and cumin seeds, add the spinach and cook until the spinach has wilted.

Using a pestle and mortar or the end of a rolling pin in a small bowl, pound the garlic with a pinch of salt.

Drain the chick peas, reserving the liquid. Stir the chick peas into the spinach with the onion mixture, the garlic mixture and ½ cup of chick pea liquid. Cover the pan and simmer for about 30 minutes, adding more liquid if necessary – the chick peas should be quite moist.
Serves 4

Overleaf:
From left to right: Catalan Noodles with Seafood, Small Filo Pastries and Chick peas with Spinach

CATALAN NOODLES WITH SEAFOOD

Pasta is an important feature of the Catalan diet: the local type, fideos, is 1-2 inches long and between vermicelli and spaghettini in thickness. It is typically cooked in a paella pan mixed with the other ingredients past the al dente stage, the cooking sometimes being completed in the oven– all of which is contrary to Italian practice.

4 CLOVES OF GARLIC, CHOPPED

1½ TABLESPOONS CHOPPED PARSLEY

4 TABLESPOONS OLIVE OIL

2 ONIONS, CHOPPED

3 TOMATOES, SKINNED, DESEEDED AND CHOPPED

1½ TEASPOONS PAPRIKA

¾ LB SCORPION FISH, MONKFISH OR HALIBUT, CUT INTO PIECES

½ LB RAW JUMBO SHRIMP IN THEIR SHELLS

½ LB RAW SHRIMP IN THEIR SHELLS

6 CUPS RICH FISH STOCK

9 OZ DRIED FIDEOS, VERMICELLI OR SPAGHETTINI BROKEN INTO SHORT LENGTHS

LARGE PINCH OF SAFFRON THREADS, CRUSHED

CHOPPED PARSLEY TO GARNISH (OPTIONAL)

TO SERVE

AIOLI (SEE PAGE 24)

LEMON WEDGES

Pound the garlic and parsley together. Heat 2 tablespoons of the oil in a cazuela or heavy flameproof earthenware casserole dish, add the onions and tomatoes, cook gently, until softened. Add the garlic and parsley mixture and paprika, continue to cook 2-3 minutes. Stir in all the seafood and coat. Add the stock, bring just to a boil, simmer gently for 5 minutes.

Meanwhile, heat the remaining oil in a large paella pan, add the fideos and stir over a moderate heat until light golden brown, but do not allow to scorch.

Remove the seafood from the cazuela and keep warm. Pour the contents of the cazuela on to the fideos, add the saffron and bring to a boil. Boil for 5 minutes, or until most of the liquid has been absorbed and the fideos are tender. Place the seafood on top, remove from the heat and leave covered by a thick cloth for a couple of minutes before sprinkling with a little parsley, if you like, and serving from the paella pan with Aïoli and lemon wedges.
Serves 4

SMALL FILO PASTRIES

Every Mediterranean country has its own version of and name for small savory pastries – "briks," "boureks/boreks," "brioutes," "sambusa" – with various different shapes and fillings. The most common are cylindrical feta cheese ones and triangular spinach and feta.

APPROXIMATELY 1 LB FILO PASTRY

OLIVE OIL FOR BRUSHING

CHEESE FILLING

¾ LB FETA CHEESE

4 TABLESPOONS CHOPPED PARSLEY AND DILL

2 EGGS, BEATEN

PEPPER

SPINACH FILLING

2 LB FRESH SPINACH, STALKS REMOVED

¼ LB EWES' MILK FETA CHEESE, CRUMBLED

FRESHLY GRATED NUTMEG

2 EGGS, BEATEN

SALT AND PEPPER

Cut each sheet of pastry into strips about 3 inches wide, stack on top of each other, cover with a damp cloth.

To make the cheese cylinders, mash the cheese with the herbs and pepper, then bind with the eggs. Brush a strip of pastry with oil, place a heaping teaspoon of filling at one end, then roll up for a few turns. Fold in the ends to seal in the filling, then continue to roll, without turning in the sides. Repeat with more strips until all the filling has been used. Place close together on a baking sheet.

To make spinach triangles, wash the spinach but do not dry, then cook in the water clinging to the leaves until wilted and surplus visible moisture has evaporated. Drain, squeeze to remove as much liquid as possible, then chop and mash with the remaining ingredients. Leave until cold.

Brush 1 of the remaining pastry strips with oil and place a heaped teaspoon of spinach filling at one end, about 1 inch from the side. Fold over one corner to make a triangle, then continue folding along the length of the pastry strip from side to side, keeping the shape of the triangle. Place side by side on a baking sheet.

Brush all the pastries with oil then bake in a preheated oven, 375°F, for 10-15 minutes, rotating the shelves as necessary, until the pastries are golden and crisp. Serve the pastries warm.

Makes about 60

MUSSEL AND TOMATO PASTRIES

The markets in the Galatasaray district of Istanbul's old commercial and diplomatic area have some of the city's best street food. The mussel stalls are always popular: they offer shelled mussels threaded on small wooden skewers, dipped in a beer batter, deep-fried and served with garlicky tarator sauce or in a split chunk of fresh white bread, with a squeeze of lemon juice or crisp, plump yufka (filo pastry) cushions filled with the succulent Turkish mussels.

24 MUSSELS, SCRUBBED AND DEBEARDED

2 TABLESPOONS OLIVE OIL, PLUS EXTRA FOR BRUSHING

3 TOMATOES, SKINNED, DESEEDED AND CUT INTO 8 PIECES EACH

1 SMALL CLOVE OF GARLIC, CRUSHED

1½ TABLESPOONS LEMON JUICE

1½ TABLESPOONS FINELY CHOPPED PARSLEY

APPROXIMATELY 2 SHEETS OF FILO PASTRY

MELTED BUTTER OR BEATEN EGG FOR GLAZING

SALT AND PEPPER

Bring about 1 inch salted water to a boil in a large saucepan. Add the mussels, cover the pan and allow the mussels to steam for 2-3 minutes, tossing the pan frequently, until the shells open. Tip the mussels into a colander and discard any that remain closed. Remove the mussels from the shells.

Heat the oil in a saucepan over a low heat, add the tomatoes and simmer until soft. Drain through a strainer, retaining the juices and reserving the tomatoes. Pour the juices back into the saucepan, add the garlic and lemon juice and boil until syrupy. Cool, then add the tomatoes, mussels and seasoning.

Stack the sheets of pastry on top of each other, brushing each with oil. Cut into twelve 4 x 4 inch squares. Wet the edges. Spoon 2 mussels with some of the sauce on to each square, then fold the pastry over and press the edges together to seal. Oil a baking sheet and place the pastries on it. Glaze the tops with melted butter or beaten egg and bake in a preheated oven, 400°F, for 10-12 minutes until golden. Carefully transfer to a wire rack. Eat the pastries warm or at room temperature.

Makes 12

PASTA WITH OLIVES, CAPERS AND ANCHOVIES

This is one of the charmingly robust, sun-packed local dishes that is served in the delightful restaurants near the port in the enchanting old town of Siracusa, the first settlement on Sicily. Sicilian cooking is based on the island's riches – fish, wheat made into memorable breads and pastas, a colorful profusion of vegetables, olives, capers, and special local cheeses, such as Pecorino Siciliano. This cheese can be eaten the day after it is made, so it is delicate, soft and creamy. Meat is not part of the Sicilian diet, but its absence passes unnoticed. The one-time Arab domination of the island is still very evident in the cooking; it is even said that "itriiya," fusilli-like corkscrew tubes of pasta, were introduced by the Muslims. Traditionally, spaghetti is used, but I prefer to use bow ties, fusilli or another shape that will catch the particles in the sauce.

¾ CUP OIL-PACKED BLACK OLIVES, PITTED AND FINELY CHOPPED

8 ANCHOVY FILLETS, RINSED, DRIED AND CHOPPED

2 TABLESPOONS CAPERS PACKED IN SALT, RINSED

4 SUN-DRIED TOMATOES, SOAKED IF NECESSARY, CHOPPED QUITE FINELY

13 OZ PASTA (SEE ABOVE)

5 TABLESPOONS VIRGIN OLIVE OIL

2 CLOVES OF GARLIC, FINELY CHOPPED

2 DRIED RED CHILES, CRUSHED

4 TABLESPOONS CHOPPED PARSLEY

SALT AND PEPPER

FRESHLY GRATED MATURE PECORINO SICILIANO OR

PECORINO SARDO CHEESE, TO SERVE

Mix together the olives, anchovies, capers, sun-dried tomatoes and black pepper.

Cook the pasta in a large saucepan in plenty of boiling salted water until just tender.

Meanwhile, heat the oil in a saucepan, add the garlic and chiles and cook until fragrant. Stir in the olive mixture and warm through.

Drain the pasta and tip into a warm serving bowl. Toss quickly with the olive mixture and the parsley and serve immediately with freshly grated Pecorino cheese.

Serves 4

ORECCHIETTE WITH PANCETTA AND BROCCOLI

Limpet shell-like orecchiette is the traditional pasta of Apulia. It is not easy to make domestically, as it is based on the local durum wheat and water, which produces a dough that is hard to work, and each piece has to be formed by hand. The shape makes it ideal for vegetable sauces.

FLORETS FROM 1 HEAD OF BROCCOLI

12 OZ FRESH OR DRIED ORECCHIETTE

3 TABLESPOONS OLIVE OIL

¼ CUP PANCETTA, DICED

2 CLOVES OF GARLIC, CRUSHED

⅓ CUP PINE NUTS

SALT AND PEPPER

FRESHLY GRATED PECORINO CHEESE TO SERVE

Cook the broccoli in boiling water for 7-8 minutes, until just tender. Drain, refresh under cold water, then drain well.

Cook the pasta in plenty of boiling salted water until just tender, 6-7 minutes for fresh, or according to the packet instructions for dried.

Meanwhile, heat the oil in a frying pan, add the pancetta and cook, stirring occasionally, until the pancetta is lightly browned, and adding the garlic towards the end. Add the nuts and heat until lightly toasted. Stir in the broccoli.

Drain the pasta, tip into a warm serving bowl and pour over the broccoli mixture. Season with salt and pepper. Toss quickly and serve with grated Pecorino cheese.

Serves 4

Top: Pasta with Olives, Capers and Anchovies
Bottom: Orecchiette with Pancetta and Broccoli

PAPPARDELLE WITH SCALLOPS AND PESTO

½ CUP *DOPPIO ZERO* FLOUR, OR UNBLEACHED STRONG OR PLAIN FLOUR

2 EGGS, BEATEN

I CLOVE OF GARLIC, CRUSHED

2 TABLESPOONS OLIVE OIL

16 SMALL SCALLOPS, OR 8 LARGE ONES, CORALS DETACHED AND WHITE BODIES CUT IN HALF HORIZONTALLY

I QUANTITY PESTO (SEE PAGE 23)

SALT AND PEPPER

I SUN-RIPENED TOMATO, DICED, SKINNED AND DESEEDED TO GARNISH

Sift the flour into a mound on a work surface and make a well in the center. Pour in the eggs, add a generous pinch of salt, then draw the flour into the eggs to form a crumbly dough, using a fork at first, then your hand, and supporting the sides of the flour to prevent the egg running out.

Lightly flour the work surface and your hands and knead the dough by pushing it away from you with the heel of one hand, folding the dough back towards you, then turning the dough through 45 degrees. Repeat for about 10 minutes until the dough is smooth and elastic, changing hands and flouring them and the surface, as necessary. Alternatively, mix the dough in a food processor. Cover the dough with an upturned bowl and leave to rest for 30 minutes.

Roll the dough away from you, on a lightly floured surface using a floured rolling pin, rotating the dough through 45 degrees in between each stroke. Continue until the dough is ⅛ inch thick. Alternatively, use a pasta machine.

Leave the rolled out dough on a clean cloth to dry for a total of 30 minutes, allowing about one third of the sheet of dough to hang over the edge of the work surface for 10 minutes before turning it so another third is hanging over for 10 minutes; repeat with remaining third. The dough is ready to cut when the surface looks leathery. Fold the pasta sheet into a loose roll, cut across into ⅛ inch strips. Alternatively, use a pasta machine. Gently open out the rolls of pappardelle and leave to dry for about 5 minutes.

Add the pappardelle to a large saucepan of boiling water, stir, cover the saucepan and bring quickly to a boil. Uncover the saucepan and boil for 4-6 minutes until just tender but firm to the bite. Meanwhile, heat the garlic in the oil in a frying pan until it is golden, then discard. Add the scallops to the remaining oil and fry for about 1 minute.

Drain the pasta and tip into a bowl, quickly add the Pesto and scallops and toss together. Serve garnished with tomato.

Serves 4

SPAGHETTI ALLA PUTTANESCA

Vibrant, racy, quick and obvious, this is a delicious pasta dish that exemplifies the character of its creators, the happy Neapolitans. "Alla puttanesca" is not the most flattering of names though – it means "in the manner of a prostitute," which is why you never see the dish given its English translation in recipes or on menus.

3 TABLESPOONS OLIVE OIL

2 CLOVES OF GARLIC, CRUSHED

I SMALL DRIED RED CHILE, DESEEDED AND CHOPPED

6 ANCHOVY FILLETS, CHOPPED

3 WELL-FLAVORED, RIPE TOMATOES, SKINNED, DESEEDED AND CHOPPED

¾ CUP PITTED BLACK OLIVES, HALVED

2 TABLESPOONS CAPERS

12 OZ DRIED SPAGHETTI

SALT

In a saucepan, heat the oil, add the garlic, chile and anchovies and cook for 1 minute. Stir in the tomatoes, olives, and capers, bring to a boil and simmer for about 20 minutes until thickened.

Cook the spaghetti in a large saucepan of boiling salted water until just tender. Drain, toss with the sauce and serve immediately.

Serves 4

FETTUCCINE VERDE WITH GORGONZOLA SAUCE

In its original form, this recipe makes a rich and luxurious dish, but a lighter version can be made by beating 4 tablespoons ricotta cheese and substituting it for the cream.

13 OUNCES FRESH OR DRIED FETTUCCINE VERDE

1 TABLESPOON OLIVE OIL

1 ONION, FINELY CHOPPED

⅓ CUP MEDIUM-BODIED DRY WHITE WINE

⅓ LB GORGONZOLA CHEESE, CHOPPED

2-3 FRESH SAGE LEAVES

½ CUP LIGHT CREAM

¼ CUP PARMESAN CHEESE, FRESHLY GRATED

SALT AND PEPPER

Bring a large saucepan of salted water to a boil, add the fettuccine, stir, cover and return to a boil. Uncover and cook until the pasta is just tender, 5-7 minutes for fresh, or according to the packet instructions for dried.

Meanwhile, heat the oil, add the onion and fry until soft. Add the wine and boil until reduced by half. Over a low heat, add the Gorgonzola and sage and stir frequently until smooth; do not allow to boil. Discard the sage and add the cream and pepper.

Drain the pasta thoroughly and return to the saucepan, pour over the sauce, toss well with the Parmesan cheese and serve immediately.

Serves 4

Variation
Fettuccine with Gorgonzola and Walnuts – omit the sage leaves and toss the cooked pasta with heaping ½ cup chopped lightly toasted walnuts. Serve sprinkled with chopped parsley.

SPAGHETTI ALLA CARBONARA

Some people say that the name "alla carbonara" is derived from the revolutionaries, called "Carbonari," who worked for the unification of Italy. Others put forward the notion that it was invented by charcoal-makers, also called "carbonari," since the ingredients were easily transportable and required very little cooking, so that the dish could be made on an open fire. The dish became internationally popular after homesick allies had "adopted" it during World War II because it contained familiar bacon and eggs rather than an Italian-style tomato sauce.

3 TABLESPOONS OLIVE OIL

½ LB PIECE OF PANCETTA, SMOKED OR GREEN, CUT INTO 1 INCH STRIPS

13 OZ SPAGHETTI

3 EGG YOLKS AND 2 WHOLE EGGS,

OR

4 WHOLE EGGS AND NO SEPARATE YOLKS

4 TABLESPOONS HEAVY CREAM OR MASCARPONE (OPTIONAL)

½ CUP PARMESAN CHEESE, FRESHLY GRATED

3 TABLESPOONS CHOPPED PARSLEY (OPTIONAL)

SALT AND PEPPER

Heat the oil in a frying pan, add the pancetta and cook, stirring occasionally, until brown and crisp.

Cook the spaghetti in plenty of boiling salted water until just tender.

Mix together the egg yolks, if using, eggs, cream or mascarpone, if using, cheese, parsley, if using, and pepper.

Drain the spaghetti, tip into a warm serving dish and immediately pour in the egg mixture and the contents of the frying pan. Toss together and serve.

Serves 4

FRAGRANT PILAF

Traditional recipes for pilafs usually specify soaking the rice, but while this may have been necessary at one time, with the rice now available I have found it makes no difference to the finished dish. Washing, however, is essential, as it removes surplus surface starch. Saffron will bring joy and happiness – or so folklore decrees – but even if it falls short on this count, it will definitely add a sunny color and its own inimitable flavor and aroma.

I CUP BASMATI RICE

SEEDS FROM 4 CARDAMOM PODS, CRUSHED

LARGE PINCH OF SAFFRON THREADS, CRUSHED (OPTIONAL)

I CINNAMON STICK

1½ TEASPOONS CUMIN SEEDS

2 BAY LEAVES

I TABLESPOON OLIVE OIL

I ONION, CHOPPED

2¼ CUPS WATER

2 TABLESPOONS LEMON JUICE

½ CUP RAISINS (OPTIONAL)

½ CUP PINE NUTS, BROWNED IN OIL

SALT AND PEPPER

Wash the rice until the water runs clear. Put the cardamom seeds, saffron, cinnamon, cumin seeds and bay leaves in a large, heavy flameproof casserole dish and dry-fry over a moderate heat for 2-3 minutes until fragrant. Add the oil and when it is hot, stir in the onion and cook gently for about 10 minutes, stirring frequently, until it has softened and lightly browned. Add the rice, turning to coat the grains in the oil. Stir in the water, lemon juice, raisins, if using, and salt and pepper. Bring to a boil, cover and simmer for 15 minutes without lifting the lid, until the rice is just tender, all the water has been absorbed and small holes puncture the surface. Remove from the heat and leave, covered, for a few minutes. Fork through the pine nuts.

Serves 4

Clockwise from bottom:
Fragrant Pilaf, Paella with Chicken
and Cannellini Bean Salad

PAELLA WITH CHICKEN

The name of the dish paella comes directly from the name of the cooking utensil in which it is cooked. The original paella (the meal) came from Valencia and was made with rabbit, chicken, snails, various beans – and no fish. In Spain, paella is a festive dish and at the slightest excuse, families and groups of friends will hightail it to the country or beach for an al fresco paella party – the ideal way to cook and enjoy a paella. An even heat under the whole surface of the base of the pan, preferably with some flames lapping slightly up the sides as they actually do affect the cooking (though perhaps this is making too fine a point), produces the best results. It is difficult to cook a paella for a number of people indoors – for 4-5 people you will need a 16 inch paella pan, for 6-8 a 20 inch one. It is very difficult to achieve the correct heat, as it is impossible to get the right even distribution of heat beneath the pan.

4 TABLESPOONS OLIVE OIL

2 LB CHICKEN, CUT INTO SMALL PIECES

4 SMALL RABBIT PORTIONS

2 SPANISH ONIONS, CHOPPED

4 CLOVES OF GARLIC, CHOPPED

I TABLESPOON PAPRIKA

1½ CUPS VALENCIAN OR RISOTTO RICE

3 EXTRA LARGE SUN-RIPENED TOMATOES, SKINNED, DESEEDED AND CHOPPED

3¾ CUPS BOILING CHICKEN STOCK

I SPRIG OF ROSEMARY

LARGE PINCH OF SAFFRON THREADS, FINELY CRUSHED

I CUP GREEN BEANS, CUT INTO SHORT LENGTHS

¾ CUP FAVA BEANS

SALT AND PEPPER

Heat the oil in a 16 inch paella pan or 9 pint wide shallow casserole dish. Add the chicken and rabbit, cook until lightly browned. Stir in the onion and garlic. Fry for 5 minutes, stir in the paprika followed by the rice. Stir 2-3 minutes, then stir in the tomatoes with all but 2 tablespoons of the stock, rosemary and salt and pepper. Dissolve the saffron in the reserved 2 tablespoons of stock, add to the paella and boil 8-10 minutes without stirring.

Scatter the green beans and fava beans over the paella – do not stir. Gradually turn down the heat and simmer until the rice is tender and the liquid absorbed, 8-10 minutes. Cover the paella with a thick cloth, remove from the heat and leave for 5-10 minutes.

Serves 4

RICE WITH FAVA BEANS

Cooking fresh fava beans and some of the cilantro along with the rice gives this Egyptian dish its special flavor, but if this ideal is not possible, the recipe can be made using thawed frozen fava beans. If you are using these, quickly add them to the rice after it has been cooking for 10 minutes and immediately cover the saucepan again.

I CUP BASMATI RICE

6 SCALLIONS, CUT INTO I INCH LENGTHS

2 TABLESPOONS OLIVE OIL

2 CUPS SHELLED FAVA BEANS

2¼ CUPS WATER

4 TABLESPOONS CHOPPED CILANTRO

SALT AND PEPPER

SPLIT ALMONDS, TOASTED, TO GARNISH

GREEK EWES' MILK YOGURT TO SERVE

Rinse the rice until the water runs clear.

Meanwhile, gently cook the scallions in the oil in a heavy saucepan, stirring, for 2-3 minutes.

Add the rice and beans and cook, stirring, until the rice is transparent. Stir in the water, half the cilantro and salt and pepper. Bring to a boil, then cover tightly and simmer for about 15 minutes, without lifting the lid, until the rice is tender and the liquid almost absorbed. Remove from the heat and leave, covered, for a few minutes. Fork through the remaining cilantro and serve garnished with toasted almonds and accompanied by yogurt.

Serves 4

POLENTA

Golden yellow polenta, made from coarsely ground cornmeal, used to be a staple food of the poor in northern Italy. Traditionally, a large copper pot, a paiolo, was kept above the open fire, specifically for cooking polenta, and a spoon was kept for stirring the porridge-like mass during the long, slow cooking process. The authentic way of adding raw polenta to the liquid is in a thin stream, but as this runs the risk of becoming lumpy, I usually blend the meal with water first. To eliminate the very frequent stirring needed during cooking, the cooking can be done in a water bath. "Instant" polenta that is ready in about 5 minutes is also available. Cheese such as Parmesan, mozzarella or fontina, and butter can be mixed in at end of cooking, if you like, and the polenta served as it is with meat, poultry or Italian sausages. It may be spread in a baking dish, cooled then baked with a topping of cheese, sliced and toasted or fried and spread with pesto or tapenade.

I½ CUPS POLENTA

6 CUPS WATER

UNSALTED BUTTER AND/OR PARMESAN CHEESE TO TASTE AND

ACCORDING TO HOW THE POLENTA IS TO BE SERVED

SALT AND PEPPER

Mix together the polenta and about I cup water. Bring the remaining water to a boil in a heavy saucepan. Stir in the polenta paste. Keep stirring until the mixture comes to the boil again, then cook, stirring very frequently, until the mixture comes away from the saucepan; this will take about 25 minutes. Place the saucepan in another saucepan filled with boiling water, cover and cook, stirring occasionally, for 30-45 minutes, or until the polenta thickens.

Add butter and/or Parmesan cheese, and season to taste.

To cut polenta into shapes for broiling or frying, spread it to a depth of about ½ -¾ inches in a shallow dish that has been rinsed with cold water. Leave until cold and set, then cut into the required shapes and either brush with olive oil and broil until a crust forms, or fry in butter.

Serves 4

Variation

Gorgonzola Polenta Crostini – mash ¼ lb Gorgonzola cheese with ¼ cup mascarpone, spread over polenta slices, broil until just bubbling, about 2 minutes, sprinkle with chopped toasted walnuts and serve hot.

RISOTTO IN BIANCO

This method has been devised perfectly to match the local rice, a medium grain one that absorbs liquid and so swells when cooked without becoming mushy. The prime rice to look for is carnaroli, but arborio is the one you are most likely to find. Risottos can be flavored with many different ingredients, but all follow the procedure given below.

I ONION, FINELY CHOPPED

I TABLESPOON UNSALTED BUTTER

1¼ CUPS CARNAROLI OR ARBORIO RICE

4½ CUPS GOOD QUALITY STOCK, BROUGHT TO A BOIL

½ CUP PARMESAN CHEESE, FRESHLY GRATED

SALT (OPTIONAL)

GRATED PARMESAN CHEESE TO SERVE (OPTIONAL)

In a heavy saucepan, cook the onion in half of the butter until translucent. Stir in the rice with a wooden spoon and cook, stirring, for 1-2 minutes until it is well coated and has absorbed the butter. Over a moderate heat, stir in about ½ cup of the boiling stock and continue to cook at a steady, but not too violent bubble, stirring constantly, until there is no free liquid and the rice is creamy. Stir in a further ½ cup or so of the boiling stock, but do not drown the rice. Continue to cook the risotto, adding gradually smaller quantities of the boiling stock until the rice is soft outside but firm within, creamy and bound together, neither moist nor dry; this should take about 15-20 minutes altogether.

Remove the pan from the heat, stir in the remaining butter, diced, and the cheese. Cover and leave 1 minute for the butter to be absorbed. Stir, taste and add salt, if necessary. Serve immediately with extra cheese, if you like.
Serves 4

Variations
Risotto with Zucchini and Thyme – use 1 small onion, 1 tablespoon unsalted butter, 1 cup rice, 2 cups stock plus 2 sliced small zucchini, 1 sprig of thyme and ¼ cup dry white wine; add the wine just before the end of the cooking.
Asparagus Risotto – add ¾ lb cooked asparagus spears, cut into ½ inch lengths, and use the asparagus cooking liquid as part of the stock for cooking the rice. Incorporate the asparagus into the rice with the last addition of stock.

BURGHUL PILAF WITH EGGPLANT AND CHEESE

Burghul pilafs can be made more quickly and easily than their rice counterpart, and make an interesting change. This is one of my favorites.

I EGGPLANT, CUT INTO I INCH CUBES

2 TABLESPOONS OLIVE OIL

1⅓ CUPS BURGHUL

I CUP WATER

½ CUP HALUMI CHEESE, CUT INTO SMALL CUBES

SALT AND PEPPER

CILANTRO LEAVES OR SHREDDED BASIL TO GARNISH

Put the eggplant into a colander, sprinkle with salt and leave for 30-60 minutes. Rinse well and pat dry.

Heat the oil, add the eggplant and fry for several minutes until tender, stirring occasionally. Using a slotted spoon, transfer to paper towels to drain.

Pour the oil from the pan. Add the burghul and water to the pan, cover and simmer for 5 minutes.

Stir in the eggplant and heat through, covered, for a few minutes. Scatter the cheese over the top, grind over black pepper, cover the pan and leave off the heat for a few minutes so the cheese begins to melt.

Serve immediately, garnished with cilantro or, unconventionally, basil.
Serves 4

SPANOKOPITTA

A good version of this typical, popular Greek pie has crisp pastry, although not too much in relation to the filling.

2 TABLESPOONS OLIVE OIL, PLUS EXTRA FOR BRUSHING

1 ONION, FINELY CHOPPED

1 BUNCH SCALLIONS, FINELY CHOPPED

2 LB FRESH SPINACH, STALKS REMOVED

2 LARGE EGGS, BEATEN

¾ CUP EWES' MILK FETA CHEESE, CRUMBLED

1½ TABLESPOONS FRESHLY GRATED KEFALOTIRI OR PARMESAN CHEESE

3 TABLESPOONS CHOPPED PARSLEY

1½ TABLESPOONS CHOPPED DILL

APPROXIMATELY 10 SHEETS FILO PASTRY

SALT AND PEPPER

Heat the oil, add the onion and scallions and cook, stirring occasionally, until softened but not colored. Wash but do not dry the spinach, then chop and stir into the onions, cook until wilted and all visible liquid has evaporated.

Remove from the heat, cool slightly and stir in the eggs, cheeses, parsley, dill, plenty of black pepper and a little salt, if necessary – the cheeses are salty anyway.

Brush a 11 x 7 inch baking pan with oil. Line with a sheet of filo, trimming it so it overhangs by 1-2 inches. Brush with oil then cover with another sheet of filo. Repeat with 3 more sheets of filo. Cover the unused sheets of filo with a damp cloth. Add the spinach mixture to the dish and spread it evenly to the sides. Layer the remaining filo in the dish as before, trimming the pastry edges to fit the dish exactly. Fold the corners and edges of the bottom pastry sheets over the top and brush well with oil or butter to seal. Brush the top generously with oil and score through the top 2 or 3 layers of pastry with the point of a sharp knife to make a diamond pattern.

Bake in a preheated oven, 350°F, for about 40 minutes until crisp and golden. Serve warm or at room temperature – do not chill.

Serves 4

Variation

Turkish Leek Pie – for the filling, substitute 4 plump leeks for the spinach. Halve the leeks lengthways, sprinkle sparingly with a little salt and leave in a colander for about 20 minutes until the leeks are limp. Squeeze well to expel surplus moisture. Mix with the eggs, cheeses, 3 tablespoons chopped parsley and a pinch of hot paprika or cayenne; do not add salt because of the salt used for the leeks.

GREEK ZUCCHINI PICNIC PIE

On the Greek islands, large picnics and family gatherings are de rigeur after Mass on Easter Sunday and Monday. Portable pastries, such as this recipe, are an obvious choice for these occasions. The yogurt and light olive oil in this pastry make it crisp and light with a delicious flavor (and, incidentally, ideal for anyone worried about cholesterol). Add a well-matched filling of zucchini, cheese and herbs and you have a pie that any true Greek would be delighted to take to the picnic.

¾ CUP ALL-PURPOSE FLOUR SIFTED WITH 1 TEASPOON BAKING POWDER

6 TABLESPOONS GREEK STRAINED EWES' MILK YOGURT

4 TABLESPOONS OLIVE OIL PLUS EXTRA FOR BRUSHING

SALT AND PEPPER

FILLING

8 SMALL ZUCCHINI, COARSELY GRATED

1 ONION, COARSELY GRATED

2 CLOVES OF GARLIC, CHOPPED

2 TABLESPOONS OLIVE OIL

¼ LB GREEK MIZITHRA CHEESE, OR EWES' MILK FETA CHEESE

4 EGGS, LIGHTLY BEATEN

½ CUP KEFALOTIRI OR PARMESAN CHEESE, FRESHLY GRATED

4 TABLESPOONS MIXED CHOPPED PARSLEY, DILL AND MINT

Toss the zucchini with salt, put in a colander, cover with a weighted plate and leave for 1 hour to drain.

To make the pastry, sift the flour and a little salt and pepper into a bowl. Make a well in the center, slowly add the yogurt and olive oil, stirring in the seasoned flour to make a smooth dough. Cover and leave in the refrigerator for 15 minutes.

Rinse the zucchini, dry well and sauté with the onion and garlic in the oil until just softened. Mix with the remaining filling ingredients.

Oil a 9 inch loose-bottomed, deep tart pan or springform pan. On a lightly floured surface, roll out the dough and use to line the pan. Prick the base with a fork and line with wax paper and baking beans. Bake in a preheated oven, 400°F, for 10-15 minutes. Lower the oven temperature to 375°F. Remove the beans and wax paper from the pastry case.

Stir the filling, pour into the pastry and bake for about 25 minutes until the filling is just set and lightly browned. Serve warm or cold.

Serves 6

Bread

Each country has its own repertoire of bread recipes. When making any of the following recipes, except pita bread, you can imitate the conditions of a traditional brick oven by baking the bread on either a baking stone or unglazed quarry tiles – inexpensive and easily available from a builder's merchant. The baking stones or quarry tiles must be preheated for at least 15 minutes before the dough is transferred to the stone or tiles, using a floured "peel" or paddle or a sheet of thin, but firm cardboard.

FOCACCIA

Originally Focaccia was baked on a stone or terracotta slab under hot ashes in the hearth. Later the dough was baked in large copper tins in a brick oven with glowing twigs surrounding the tin. Focaccia may be flavored in many different ways, whether crackling with crunchy coarse salt, studded with black olives, almost oozing with rich-flavored olive oil, scented with herbs, topped with melting, savory onions or combined with crisp diced bacon. In the fishing village of Recco, between Genoa and Santa Margherita, the local soft cows' cheese is sandwiched between two layers of dough, the top one being so thin it is almost transparent. There are also some sweet versions. Focaccia is eaten as a snack, served as antipasti with cheese or to accompany a meal, and is ideal for picnics. Because of the oil it contains, the dough is easy to work.

1 PACKAGE ACTIVE DRIED YEAST

APPROXIMATELY 1¼ CUPS WARM MILK

4 CUPS UNBLEACHED ALL-PURPOSE WHITE FLOUR

3-5 TABLESPOONS VIRGIN OLIVE OIL, PLUS EXTRA FOR BRUSHING

COARSE SEA SALT

Dissolve the yeast with the milk and leave until frothy. Sift the flour into a large bowl, stir in a little salt and make a well in the center. Slowly pour in the yeast liquid and oil, stirring the dry ingredients into the liquid to make a smooth, soft but not wet dough; add a little more milk if necessary. Turn on to a floured surface and knead until smooth and elastic. Place the dough in a clean bowl, cover and leave at room temperature until doubled in bulk.

Flour a baking sheet. Tip the dough on to a floured surface and knead for 2-3 minutes. Roll the dough into a large circle about ¼-½ inch thick – the thicker it is, the chewier the bread. Carefully transfer the dough to the baking sheet, keeping the circular shape. Brush with olive oil and sprinkle over coarse salt. With the end of a wooden spoon or a clean finger make deep indentations over the surface of the dough. Spray with water and leave until doubled in bulk. Put the bakestone or quarry tiles, if using, and a baking pan in the oven to heat for 20 minutes.

Transfer the loaf to the bakestone or quarry tiles, if using. Put the loaf in a preheated oven, 400°F, and fill the baking pan with hot water. Immediately close the oven door and bake the loaf for 15-20 minutes if ¼ inch thick, 20-25 minutes if slightly thicker, until golden and the underneath sounds hollow when tapped. Serve warm.

Serves 4

Variations

Focaccia with Herbs – knead 10 or 12 torn fresh sage leaves or 2 teaspoons rosemary leaves into the dough at the second kneading. Shape and leave to rise as before, brush with an extra tablespoon of olive oil before baking.

Focaccia with Sun-dried Tomatoes – add about 2 large chopped sun-dried tomatoes kept in oil to the dough before the final shaping; use the oil from the tomatoes in the dough.

Gorgonzola Focaccia – add ⅓ lb chopped Gorgonzola cheese to the dough before the final shaping.

Cheese-Filled Focaccia – after the second rising, halve the dough; use 1 piece to line a 15 x 10 inch oiled baking pan, leaving a slight overhang. Cover the surface with 1 lb sliced stracchino or other soft melting cheese, leaving a 1 inch border. Cover with the remaining dough, folding the bottom overhang over to seal the edge. Sprinkle with coarse salt, then bake for 30 minutes at 400°F. Cool for 5 minutes before cutting.

Tomato and Anchovy-Filled Focaccia – soften 2 chopped onions and 2 garlic cloves in olive oil, but do not allow to color. Add 5 skinned, deseeded and chopped sun-ripened tomatoes, 4 sun-dried tomato halves, 2 tablespoons capers and 1 tablespoon oregano and simmer until thick. Let cool. Roll out half the dough to a 12 inch circle, place on an oiled baking sheet and spread with the tomato mixture, leaving a 1 inch border. Arrange 12 anchovy fillets on top, scatter over ½ cup pitted oil-cured black olives, then 1½ cups coarsely grated mozzarella. Cover with the remaining dough and seal the edges. Bake at 425°F for 30 minutes until risen and golden. Serve warm.

Clockwise from top right:
Goats' Cheese, Tomato and Pesto Pizza,
Focaccia and Pissaladière

PIZZA

In colloquial Italian, a "pizza" is almost any kind of pie, savory or sweet, open or covered and made from any type of pastry or yeast dough. The concept of adding savory ingredients to bread dough has been around since the earliest days of breadmaking, but the pizza as we know it today was the creation of the Neopolitans during the eighteenth century, when they added a layer of the tomatoes that were doing so well there. Italian pizzas vary in depth, getting thicker as you travel northwards. Pizza dough is given just one rising to produce its characteristic compact and resilient consistency.

1½ CUPS UNBLEACHED ALL-PURPOSE WHITE FLOUR

¼ TEASPOON SALT

½ PACKAGE ACTIVE DRY YEAST

APPROXIMATELY 1 CUP WARM WATER

1 TABLESPOON OLIVE OIL

Sift the flour and salt into a bowl, stir in the yeast and form a well in the center. Slowly pour in the warm water and the oil, stirring the dry ingredients into the liquids with your hands to make a wet dough. Beat for 2-3 minutes then turn on to a floured surface and knead for about 5 minutes or until the dough becomes smooth and elastic. Transfer to a bowl, cover with a clean cloth and leave in a warm place for about 1 hour until doubled in bulk.

Put the bakestone or quarry tiles, if using, in the oven to heat for 20 minutes and flour a paddle or sheet of cardboard, or oil a baking sheet.

Turn the dough on to a floured surface, knead for 2-3 minutes, then roll to a circle about 10 inches in diameter, making the edges slightly thicker than the center. Carefully transfer the dough to the paddle, cardboard or baking sheet, keeping the circular shape. The pizza base is now ready to cover with your chosen topping.

Transfer the prepared pizza to the bakestone or quarry tiles, if using, and bake in a preheated oven, 425°F, for about 20 minutes until the pizza is risen and the outside rim and the base is crisp and golden.

PIZZA TOPPINGS

Roasted Sweet Red Pepper and Black Olive – 1 quantity pizza base. Finely chop ¾ cup pitted black olives with ½ small onion and 1 clove of garlic. Slowly mix in 2 tablespoons olive oil. Add black pepper to taste then spread evenly over the pizza base, right to the edges. Scatter over 3 charred and sliced sweet red peppers, sprinkle with 1½ cups coarsely grated mozzarella cheese and a few black olives. Sprinkle the baked pizza with torn basil and a chopped red onion.
Serves 2

Caramelized Onion, Gorgonzola and Walnut – 1 quantity pizza dough. Gently soften, brown and lightly caramelize 1 lb chopped and salted Spanish onions in a little unsalted butter and olive oil in a heavy frying pan. Stir in 1 tablespoon finely chopped rosemary, let cool, then spread the onions over the dough right to the edges. Sprinkle with pepper and scatter over 1 cup chopped Gorgonzola cheese and ½ cup chopped walnuts.
Serves 2

Artichoke and Mushroom – add a squeeze of lemon juice to the oil from 13 ounces artichokes in oil and brush over the pizza base. Slice the artichokes in half. Sauté ¼ lb sliced oyster mushrooms in olive oil, toss with the artichokes and distribute evenly over the base. Scatter over 1 cup grated fontina cheese. Sprinkle the baked pizza with chopped marjoram and serve.
Serves 2

Goats' Cheese, Tomato and Pesto – spread with Pesto (see page 23), cover with thinly sliced well-flavoured tomatoes, then scatter over about 1¼ cups crumbled goats' cheese, trickle with virgin olive oil. Garnish the baked pizza with basil leaves, if you like.
Serves 2

GREEK SWEET EASTER BREAD

This braided loaf with hard-boiled eggs – dyed red and polished with olive oil – nestling in it, is just one of the many sweet things that are made to celebrate a festival, in this case the ending of the 40-day Lenten fast. On the islands, the breads are the traditional gift from children to their godparents, who hang them on their walls for decoration on Easter day before eating them. In Greece, red-dyed eggs are purported to have protective powers and packages of them are sold at every pavement kiosk and general store for weeks before Easter. Similar eggs can easily be prepared by hard boiling eggs in water colored dark red with a few drops of dark red edible food coloring.

For the finest texture, the dough should be left to rise several times. The loaf may also be decorated with blanched almonds and sesame or caraway seeds.

3 TABLESPOONS LUKEWARM WATER

I CUP LUKEWARM MILK

4 CUPS ALL-PURPOSE WHITE FLOUR

GRATED RIND OF I ORANGE

I PACKAGE ACTIVE DRY YEAST

OIL FOR BRUSHING

6 TABLESPOONS UNSALTED BUTTER, SOFTENED

¾ CUP SUGAR

2 EGGS, BEATEN

3 RED-DYED EGGS (SEE ABOVE)

I BEATEN EGG YOLK FOR GLAZING

2 TABLESPOONS SPLIT ALMONDS

Add the water to the milk. Stir together the flour, orange rind and yeast in a large bowl. Mix the liquid into the dry ingredients to form a smooth dough, and then knead the dough until it is soft, pliable and elastic.

Brush a bowl with oil, place the dough in it, cover and leave at room temperature until doubled in bulk.

Turn the dough on to a lightly floured surface and knead lightly and briefly. Repeat the rising to make a loaf with a finer texture. Alternatively, you can omit the second rising.

While the dough is rising, beat together the unsalted butter and sugar in a bowl until creamy. Gradually beat in the eggs.

Tip the dough on to the work surface, lightly pinch in the butter mixture, then knead briefly to incorporate evenly.

Divide the dough into 3 equal pieces then roll out each piece to a long strand about the thickness of a sausage and tapered at both ends. Dampen one end of each strand and press these ends together, then braid the strands, incorporating the hard-boiled, red-dyed eggs at even intervals. Carefully transfer the loaf to an oiled baking sheet and leave until doubled in bulk.

Brush the top of the loaf with beaten egg yolk and sprinkle over the almonds. Bake in a preheated oven, 400°F, for 30-35 minutes until golden brown on top and the bottom sounds hollow when tapped. Let cool on a wire rack.

Makes I loaf

Desserts & Cakes

The legendary Middle Eastern sweet tooth is shared by the Turks and Greeks. The very sweet recipes for which they are renowned are eaten, not at the end of a meal, but with coffee or on special occasions. Indeed many have particular religious or festive associations. Fruit is the more usual end to a meal and home made desserts tend to be simple and homely, such as rice pudding. More complicated dishes, special pastries and cakes will more often be bought from the baker's rather than prepared at home.

ALMOND PASTRY SNAKE

The Moroccan name for this rich, lightly perfumed pastry, "M'hanncha," means "the snake," accurately describing its coiled shape. The snake will keep for several days if stored in an airtight container in a cool place, but not the refrigerator. Reheat gently before serving, if you like.

2 CUPS GROUND ALMONDS

1½ CUPS CONFECTIONERS' SUGAR

1 EGG, SEPARATED

FEW DROPS OF ALMOND ESSENCE

1½ TABLESPOONS ROSE WATER

CONFECTIONERS' SUGAR FOR SPRINKLING

6 SHEETS OF FILO PASTRY

4 TABLESPOONS OLIVE OIL

TO DECORATE

CONFECTIONERS' SUGAR

GROUND CINNAMON

Stir the ground almonds and confectioners' sugar together and mix to a paste with the egg white, almond essence and rose water. Divide into 3 equal pieces. Sift confectioners' sugar over the work surface then roll out each piece of almond paste to a 19 inch long "sausage," about ½ inch thick.

Brush a sheet of filo pastry with oil, cover with a second sheet of pastry and brush that with oil; cover the unused pastry with a damp cloth. Place one almond "sausage" along the length of the oiled pastry, about 1 inch from the edge. Roll up the pastry, enclosing the almond "sausage." Form into a loose coil starting in the center of an oiled 8 inch round tart pan with a removeable bottom.

Repeat with the remaining almond 'sausages' and pastry. Join one to the end of the coil in the pan, continue the coil outwards, then repeat with the last piece.

Beat the egg yolk with a pinch of ground cinnamon and brush over the top. Bake in a preheated oven, 350°F, for about 30 minutes until golden and crisp on top.

Remove the sides of the pan, carefully turn the coil over, return to the base of the pan and place in the oven for a further 10 minutes until the bottom is brown. Invert on to a cooling rack and let cool slightly. Sift over confectioners' sugar and ground cinnamon. Serve warm, cut into wedges.
Makes 12 pieces

Clockwise from right: Almond Pastry Snake, Valencian Cake and Greek Custard Pie

VALENCIAN CAKE

Oranges and almonds were both introduced to the Valencian area of Spain by the Arabs and are still important crops – both in the cooking and as a valuable export. The sweetness and flavor of the oranges and the freshness of the almonds will make all the difference to whether this is just a good, moist cake with a lingering orange flavor or a very special one. Pounding the nuts gives a more interesting texture, but if you feel this is too laborious, use half ground almonds and half finely chopped almonds. I recommend waiting for a day before eating the cake, as it will be even better.

1 CUP BLANCHED ALMONDS

4 EGGS, SEPARATED

1½ CUPS SUGAR

GRATED RIND AND JUICE OF 3 ORANGES

1 CINNAMON STICK, BROKEN IN HALF

1 TABLESPOON ORANGE LIQUEUR (OPTIONAL)

Butter and flour an 8 inch round non-stick or spring-form cake pan. Pound the almonds in a mortar using a pestle until reduced to coarse crumbs.

Whisk the egg yolks and 1 cup of the sugar until thick, then stir in the orange rind and almonds. Using a clean whisk, whisk the egg whites until stiff but not dry. Fold one third of the egg whites into the almond mixture until just evenly mixed, then add the remaining egg whites in two batches in the same way. Spoon into the cake pan and bake in a preheated oven, 350°F, for 45 minutes until golden and set in the center. Do not worry if the cake rises then deflates again. Let cool a little, then transfer to a deep serving plate.

Heat the remaining sugar in the orange juice with the cinnamon stick, stirring until the sugar has dissolved, then boil for a couple of minutes. Remove from the heat, add the liqueur, if using, then slowly pour the syrup over the entire top of the cake until it has all been absorbed.
Serves 6-8

GREEK CUSTARD PIE

This is a lighter version of baklava. If the sweetness of this recipe is not to your liking, adjust to taste.

8 SHEETS OF FILO PASTRY

MELTED UNSALTED BUTTER FOR BRUSHING

ROSE OR ORANGE FLOWER WATER TO SERVE (OPTIONAL)

FILLING

4 CUPS MILK

I CINNAMON STICK

I CUP SUGAR

7 TABLESPOONS FINE SEMOLINA

1½ TABLESPOONS GRATED ORANGE RIND

6 EGGS, BEATEN

SYRUP

1½ CUPS SUGAR

3 TABLESPOONS LEMON JUICE

LARGE STRIP OF FINELY PARED LEMON RIND

LARGE STRIP OF FINELY PARED ORANGE RIND

To make the filling, boil the milk with the cinnamon stick, remove from the heat, cover and leave for 30 minutes. Stir in the sugar and return to a boil. Stir in the semolina and simmer gently for about 5 minutes. Remove from the heat, remove and reserve the cinnamon stick and stir in the orange rind and the eggs. Lay a sheet of dampened wax paper on the surface, let cool completely.

Butter a 13 x 9 inch baking pan, line with 4 sheets of filo pastry, brushing each with melted butter; cover remaining filo with a damp towel. Spread filling evenly over the filo, cover with remaining pastry, buttering each sheet first. Trim the edges, score the surface into 3 inch diamonds with a sharp knife. Bake in preheated oven, 350°F, for 45-50 minutes until crisp and the filling is set. Let cool in the pan, on a wire rack.

To make the syrup, gently heat the sugar with the lemon juice, I cup water, the lemon and orange rinds and the reserved cinnamon stick, stirring until the sugar dissolves. Bring rapidly to a boil and boil for 2-3 minutes. Cover, remove from heat and leave until lukewarm. Remove the fruit rinds and cinnamon stick, slowly and carefully pour the syrup evenly over the pie and leave for the syrup to be absorbed. Serve cut into diamonds with a few drops of rose or orange flower water sprinkled over, if you like.

Serves 12

RICE PUDDING

Rice pudding is popular from Morocco to Greece – and the people in those countries really do know how to make a good rice pudding (no shades of the school lunch version). They cook the rice slowly for a long time, coaxing it into absorbing plenty of milk, so making a very creamy pudding.
Almonds are often added, giving more flavor. Traditionally, the nuts would be transformed into almond milk by pounding by hand, but nowadays it can be done by grinding the nuts in a blender, mixing in hot water, then straining the result. This is repeated once more.
The quicker and easier way is to add freshly ground almonds to the pudding, which will make it even creamier (because extra milk is needed), give more flavor and a different texture.

APPROXIMATELY 4 CUPS MILK

¼ CUP PUDDING (SHORT-GRAIN) RICE, RINSED AND DRAINED

¼ CUP SUGAR

1-1½ TABLESPOONS ORANGE FLOWER OR ROSE WATER

TO DECORATE

CHOPPED PISTACHIO NUTS OR ALMONDS

CRYSTALLIZED VIOLETS OR ROSES

Heat the milk in a heavy, preferably non-stick saucepan. Sprinkle over the rice and sugar and bring to a boil, stirring. Lower the heat and cook very gently, stirring occasionally, until the pudding is thick, velvety and falls easily from the spoon – this may take anything up to 2 hours. Use a heat diffusing mat, if necessary, to prevent the rice cooking too quickly and sticking. Stir in the orange flower water or rose water to taste.

Pour into a serving dish or individual dishes. Serve warm or cold with pistachio nuts, almonds, crystallized violets or roses scattered over.

Serves 4

PEACHES POACHED IN DESSERT WINE

A saying with much truth is that the food and wine of an area go well together. A very good example derives from the two fruits of the Languedoc soil – plump, fragrantly juicy peaches and Muscat de Lunel wine, with its luscious, delicately honeyed taste and light underlying acidity that prevents it being cloying. The combination of peaches in dessert wine works well even if the fruit and wine come from elsewhere and it is a good way of improving peaches lacking in character. The nearest substitute (in geographical as well as quality terms) for Muscat de Lunel is the more widely available Muscat de Frontignac.

2 TABLESPOONS SUGAR

1¼ CUPS MUSCAT DE LUNEL OR SIMILAR DESSERT WINE

LONG STRIP OF LEMON RIND

LONG STRIP OF ORANGE RIND

4 RIPE BUT FIRM PEACHES, HALVED AND STONED

Gently heat the sugar in the wine in a frying pan that the peach halves will just fit in a single layer, stirring until dissolved. Add the lemon and orange rinds and the peaches. Add sufficient water almost to cover the peaches, then poach until tender – 5-10 minutes depending on ripeness. Using a slotted spoon, lift the peaches from the pan, remove their skins and place the fruit, cut-side up, in a shallow serving dish.

Boil the liquid until very lightly syrupy and pour over the fruit. Let cool, cover and place in the refrigerator for about 2 hours. For a special occasion, serve the peaches topped with Ricotta Pudding (see next recipe).

Serves 4

RICOTTA PUDDING

This is an Italian pudding, "burdino," so would be more usually baked, but I prefer it uncooked when it is lighter and more delicate. Mascarpone is the most voluptuous cheese and, until recently, Italians managed to keep it to themselves, as it could be made only during the winter months and had to be eaten within a few days. However, now, the UHT process, which heats the cheese to a high temperature for a short time, has extended the shelf-life of the cheese and it can be made year round. The flavor does suffer a bit though, so if you are lucky enough to obtain unheat-treated cheese, snap it up.

⅓ CUP MIXED CANDIED CITRON PEEL AND APRICOTS, FINELY CHOPPED

1½ TABLESPOONS BRANDY OR COINTREAU

1 CUP FRESH RICOTTA CHEESE

2 EGGS, SEPARATED

¼ CUP VANILLA SUGAR

FINELY GRATED RIND OF ½ LEMON

½ CUP MASCARPONE CHEESE

½ CUP AMARETTI BISCUITS, CRUSHED

RIPE PEACHES, RASPBERRIES, STRAWBERRIES OR CHERRIES TO SERVE

Leave the candied fruits to soak in the brandy or Cointreau for 30 minutes.

Push the ricotta through a strainer into a bowl and beat in the egg yolks, sugar, lemon rind, soaked fruits and any remaining liquid. Gently fold in the mascarpone cheese.

In a clean dry bowl, whisk the egg whites until stiff but not dry, then gently fold into the ricotta mixture. Pour into a large bowl, cover and chill for 4-6 hours. Sprinkle over the amaretti just before serving with the fruit.

Serves 4

Peaches Poached in Dessert Wine
topped with Ricotta Pudding

Author's acknowledgement

During my work on the preparation of this book many
people have helped me, some knowingly, others, such as
shop-keepers and stall-holders, unknowingly. To everyone
I extend a big thankyou. To Emirates Airline and
the Dubai Hilton I offer my thanks for their
generous hospitality.

The publishers would also like to thank
the hotel, La Residencia, Mallorca
for the kind use of their facilities.